The Embodiment of Knowledge

By William Carlos Williams

† *City Lights Books*

WILLIAM CARLOS WILLIAMS

The Embodiment of Knowledge

edited with an introduction by
Ron Loewinsohn

A NEW DIRECTIONS BOOK

Copyright © 1974 by Florence H. Williams
Introduction and notes, Copyright © 1974 by Ron Loewinsohn

The material in this book was found among the William Carlos Williams papers, Collection of American Literature, Beinecke Library, Yale University, to which grateful acknowledgment is made.

Manufactured in the United States of America
First published clothbound in 1974 and as New Directions
Paperbook 434 in 1977.
Published simultaneously in Canada by Penguin Books Canada Limited

Library of Congress Cataloging in Publication Data

Williams, William Carlos, 1883–1963.
   The embodiment of knowledge.

   (A New Directions Book)
   1. Williams, William Carlos, 1883–1963—Philosophy.
2. Williams, William Carlos, 1883–1963—Language.
I. Title.
PS3545.I544Z514   1974   120   74–8568
ISBN 0–8112–0553–3
ISBN 0–8112–0647–5 pbk.

New Directions Books are published for James Laughlin
by New Directions Publishing Corporation,
80 Eighth Avenue, New York 10011

THIRD PRINTING

Contents

Acknowledgments

I want to thank James Laughlin of New Directions, Dr. Williams's friend and publisher for many years, for permission to examine the manuscripts at Yale and Buffalo, and for his suggestions and cooperation in the preparation of this edition. Mrs. Florence Williams approved the plan of the book. Donald Gallup, of the Beinecke Library at Yale, and Emily Mitchell Wallace, Williams's bibliographer, offered helpful advice. The Research Committee of the University of California, Berkeley, provided funds to prepare the final typescript. My sons, Joe and William, each helped in their way. James Breslin and Kathryn Hughes both read my introduction in various stages and drafts and offered generous and valuable criticism. Without the help of all these people this edition might have been completed, but preparing it would never have been the enjoyable and rewarding thing that it was for me.

R. L.

Introduction

DURING THE YEARS when I was going to graduate school I used to (as often as I thought I could afford it) take time off from the study of Anglo-Saxon or seminars in the Transcendentalists or Benjamin Franklin, sneak across the Charles to Boston Garden and watch Bill Russell lead the Boston Celtics against the best the National Basketball Association had to offer. Russell provided a different kind of education. At six-foot-nine he wasn't the tallest center in the league, he wasn't especially fast, his shooting average was only respectable, yet in every move he made he manifested an intelligence, both mental and physical, that enabled him to make fools of men as much as five inches taller. He had by then made himself into a myth which he proved in his own person each night he played, continuing his own revolution in the nature of professional basketball. It was a matter of timing, of position, of that complex psychology of sports that's part foreknowledge, part intimidation and part drama. Above all it was a matter of a bodily intelligence in which the fundamentals of the game and an enormous amount of data—his opponents' most likely moves, the physics of the speed and trajectory of a basketball bouncing off a steel hoop, the constantly changing position of the other nine men on the court—all that information and more has become a possession and an activity of the synapses and muscles so that there is no split between brain and limbs, and one might almost say his body thought. Watching Russell go up for a rebound against Wilt Chamberlain (seven-foot-two) and coming down with the ball, his head already jerking from side to side trying to spot an open man to pass off to even before his feet had come back down to the hardwood floor—it was as elegant as one of Chomsky's diagrams and gave a *frisson* like "The Battle of Maldon." Often too there would be flashes of a bodily wit: Russell standing in a low post with his back to the basket, the ball held high above his head, flipping it off to Havliceck cutting behind him down the lane for a layup.

Russell is a perfect embodiment of that general term, a "professional man," a man who professes or declares himself —who makes himself actual—in the activity to which he's committed. This notion of a man's profession as a process of self-actualization is a central term in William Carlos Williams's belief and in his art. "You want [your poems]," he wrote to a young poet in 1950, "you want them to be uniquely you, you in the face (and the intimacy) of the world. They are an assurance that you, yourself, exist in every final delicacy of your being." (*Letters*, 282) Earlier, in 1929, he asked himself, "Why do you write?" and answered, "For relaxation and relief. To have nothing in my head—to freshen my eye by that till I see, smell, know and can reason and be." (*Imaginations*, 289) And here, in this collection of essays, notes, fragments and jottings to which he gave the title *The Embodiment of Knowledge*, he writes of Shakespeare's language as "the deed of speeches in which a man is most real." A man, that is, like Shakespeare, who professed himself in dramatic speeches, a man whose actions, those deeds by which he took possession of his own experiences and made them actual for himself and others, are words, words that *are* actions and that speak as loudly, moving and compelling us as they inform us. And in these same pages, speaking of that total complex of perception and feeling that constitutes a painter's "subject," he says, "Render that in paint and [the artist] asserts his own existence and that of men about him."

It's right to associate Williams and Russell here because for both men self-definition is a process, an on-going activity of self-assertion characterized by contention. Both men assert themselves over against an opponent. Russell, as a competitive athlete, is an *agonist*, a participant in a conflict. Williams, late in his career, felt the struggle to assert and affirm his identity as a poet as "an agony of self-realization bound/into a whole/by that which surrounds it." (*Pictures from Brueghel*, 109) Russell, as a man, struggled against the popular stereotypes of how a black man should conduct himself, how a professional athlete (especially a black professional athlete) should relate to his public, his fans. On the court he contended not only against his opponents but also against conventions that dictated how the game and particularly his role as center should be played. Williams struggled throughout his career against similar conventions concerning poetic decorum. Especially he contended against *inherited* conventions, against the past and the ways it seeks to define us in despite of our needs and our desires.

> There is an antagonism between the ages. Each age wishes to enslave the others. Each wishes to succeed. It is very human and completely understandable . . . If we read alone [*i.e.,* without writing] we are somehow convinced that we are not quite alive, that we are somehow less than they —who lived before us . . .
>   Fixed in words—in the very classics are many—most— if not all of the stupidities which enthrall us, which make us want to write, which inspire us to break out. To read, while we are imbibing the wisdom of the ages, we are at the same time imbibing the death and the imbecility, the enslaving rudeness of the ages.
>   WE are the center of the writing, each man for himself but at the same time each man for his own age first.

But isn't Williams here concerned as much with continuities as with disjunctions or antagonisms? Each age sets itself against the others, but insofar as they all do that aren't they all alike? Each individual man as he reads the classics of a previous age (and where, except in Hollywood or Madison Avenue, do we hear of *contemporary* "classics"?) feels a similar paradox of enslavement and liberation. "WE" are the center of the writing because it's each individual reader's experience of simultaneous enthrallment and freedom that defines the classics as such. The individual reader. In his absence a work can't have a summative or cultural value. It's only as we, individually, discover a work's perfections and as we discover ourselves in it that a work comes to be felt as a classic.

Implicit in Williams's notion of the reader as the center of the writing in his own present as he reads is the assumption that discovery is a process, that education and knowledge are on-going activities in which we create ourselves from day to day. And in fact, this on-going quality of education is implicit in the word's etymology. *Education* derives from the Latin *duco, ducere*, "to lead," together with the prefix *e-*, "out." To educate the student is to lead him out—but out of what? Out of himself, we suppose, but what, then, is he being led into? Well, out into the world at large. But neither of those terms, neither the student's self nor the world at large, is a static quantity. They are both most accurately characterized as processes.

Knowledge itself, which Williams seeks to *embody* in at least two senses in these notes—knowledge itself is a process, not something acquired or achieved permanently at the end of an arduous pursuit. Above all, since he conceives of knowledge as a continuing activity, Williams rejects that metaphor of a *field* of knowledge which we often find in college catalogues, a "field" as a circumscribed quantity of knowledge ("science," say, or "philosophy") which is progressively disclosed until we have acquired a complete and permanent understanding of it.

> What vista does philosophy bring to mind?
> Is it not a field partly known which when finally we have accomplished the design we shall know all?
> Nothing could be more false—stultifying. For what of fields beyond that—and other fields?
> But it is false far and above even that base. Nothing more stultifying. It is responsible—more than death . . . for

the postponement of knowledge of life which is a major
predicament of the mind today. It *will* be when—etc. etc.
. . . To know is everywhere, teeming, at once, in any-
thing.

Science and philosophy, in Williams's conception of
them, imagine some time, some misty future in which all
phenomena will be explained, ideally with a pocketful of
formulae which can all be derived from each other, some
dialectic, perhaps, or some inverse-square law, or some
primal reflex-arc located, perhaps, in the pineal gland. In the
meantime we all walk around feeling ourselves incomplete,
partially empty. Knowledge so defined dehumanizes us both
as we lack it and as we "acquire" it: having it we leave our
fellow humans behind us, lacking it we look ahead self-
deprecatingly. I think here of all those students who have
sat in my office, looking disconsolately at the books on my
shelves (how many of them have *I* read?), saying, "I feel
so stupid, well, not stupid but ignorant. There's so much
I don't know."

Williams answers this hopelessness by pointing out the
"scientific-philosophic mistake," which is to place

> a mythical end to research at some remote future—toward
> which striving was inaugurated—comparable to a very
> identical "heaven" of mystical understanding.

Elsewhere in this volume he makes it clear that "knowledge
is not at the end of the deduction but in each phase of it and
everywhere." In these notes he sets himself against the char-
acter Henry Adams creates in his *Education of Henry
Adams*, who is always seeking an *ultimate* knowledge or
education, and so missing the integrity of his life as he's
living it. (Where the *author* of the *Education of Henry
Adams* is in this recurring disappointment is another matter
altogether.)

Williams himself was of course not a philosopher. He
doesn't systematically elaborate the notions he postulates.

But his ideas are extremely provocative. They place him in a line of development that includes William James, Dewey and Whitehead, and they anticipate by some forty years statements by Jean Piaget, who does elaborate them and support them with empirical evidence. (See especially Piaget's *Psychology and Epistemology*, N.Y. 1971.)

And if knowledge is a process, an on-going activity, it follows that man's conception of his world and of his place in it will be characterized by mysteries, doubts, uncertainties. The question is, are we going to accept this condition as a doom or a blessing, as a stricture or a possibility? Keats, whom Williams took for his first master, said that the crucial quality that went to form a man of achievement, especially in literature, was the capability to proceed in the face of such "uncertainties, mysteries, doubts, without any irritable reaching after fact and reason." Williams had this "negative capability" in abundance, and he proposed it as the most humane orientation toward knowledge. "Man must give himself without complete knowledge in the world—or he will not give himself at all. That is to say he will know—in his body—nothing at all."

Williams then associates knowing somehow with giving. It's characterized by generosity rather than acquisitiveness as, say, in Faust, for whom knowledge is power. And knowledge is not an escape from ignorance, as if that were an enclosed field whose fence we leap over to *arrive* at knowing. Rather, the two are both partial, processes that qualify each other.

> It [this humane orientation toward knowledge which is anterior to all systems of thought] is the past (from which man has come). It is the "night mind," the chaos, the source of religion; the pre-conscious, the savage, the animal, the plant, the inorganic—what you will.
> But it is none of these. It is one: all tentatives fit into it, not it into them. It is particularly not "the past" out of which knowledge or consciousness going "up" proceeds, leaving it behind. It exists co-incidentally with consciousness, systems, is not escaped.

Further, knowledge, knowing, is not merely an abstraction, a mental process, but has a physical aspect as well. "Man must give himself without complete knowledge in the world—or . . . he will know—*in his body*—nothing at all." This *embodiment* of knowledge is one of the primary threads that tie this seemingly scattered collection of notes together. Williams is here attempting to *humanize* knowledge by stressing the fact that, to be truly useful to us as individuals and as members of the human race, knowledge must be seen as having a body, an immediate concreteness which we apprehend sensorily before we can usefully assimilate it. Any student who has tried to study for an exam by reading plot outlines rather than the works themselves will testify to the poverty of such abstract "learning." It's like trying to substitute a menu for the meal itself. The same is true for the chemistry lab, where the knowledge gained takes on a physical immediacy which the lectures lacked. So much depends upon the concrete thing itself which we relate to always in a specific location, whether in the present or in our memory—a red wheelbarrow, a dish of plums, an industrial city in north Jersey. No knowledge without a body; "Say it, no ideas but in things."

And Williams's title, rich thing that it is, moves simultaneously in another direction. If knowledge has a bodily aspect in itself, it must also, before it can be fully, humanely, useful, be assimilated into the total organism, into the body as well as the mind. As early as 1917 or 1918, in *Kora in Hell*, Williams was aware of this.

> That which is known has value only by virtue of the dark. This cannot be otherwise. A thing known passes out of the mind into the muscles, the will is quit of it, save only when set into vibration by the forces of darkness opposed to it.
>
> (*Imaginations*, 74)

The fundamentals of the game of basketball have passed out of Bill Russell's mind as he sets himself against an opposing player, into his muscles. He doesn't *will* himself to leap at precisely that moment to block that shot, yet his body manifests an intelligence that's equal to, even if different from, his judgment. Bill Williams, incidentally, was a physician who turned to poetry, he tells us, after his doctors told him that a life of competitive sports wouldn't be a possibility for him. (He'd collapsed on the track field at Horace Mann High School as a teen-ager, after overexerting himself. His condition was diagnosed as "adolescent heart strain.") By the time he gets to page three of this collection he's already talking about football coaches, and throughout his autobiographical writings Williams is concerned with physical excellence, not only in high school and college athletes, but also in his own person, his own hands, whose coordination with (rather than subordination to) his mind was so obviously crucial as he practiced medicine. He would have been pleased, I think, with Norman Mailer's account of the Muhammad Ali–Joe Frazier championship fight, in which Mailer points out that Ali's combinations of lefts and rights demonstrate a wit comparable to anything in Pope or Wycherly. And Williams's notion of the assimilation of knowledge into the body anticipates Gestalt psychology.

> A theory which you have mastered—digested in detail so that you have made it yours—can be used flexibly and efficiently because it has become "second nature" to you. But some "lesson" which you have swallowed whole without comprehension—for example, "on authority"—and which you now have to use "as if" it were your own, is an introject. . . . Learning, when it is digested and not swallowed whole, is said to be assimilated; it can then be used not otherwise than one's muscularity.
> (Perls, Hefferline and Goodman, *Gestalt Therapy,*
> N.Y., 1971, Delta Edition, 189-90, 421.)

If ideas, knowledge, have such a physicality, it's in part because words themselves are characterized by a bodyness of which we aren't often aware, we're so intent on the ideas or objects which the words are supposed to convey, as if we could discard the words as soon as they complete their function as *vehicles* for the transportation of ideas. Little disposable station wagons. We aren't often enough mindful that words have qualities of their own, qualities which affect our perception of and response to the total complex of words-and-referent. (Dante called various words "shaggy" or "buttered" according to their sound.) Williams most often, in this collection and elsewhere, condemns science and philosophy for using words only as vehicles for conveying meaning. But once in a while he can be explicit about the various ways language is used—in science and philosophy, and in poetry.

> Language is . . . divided according to its use into two main phases. 1. That by which it is made secondary to the burden of ideas—information, what not—for service to philosophy, science, journalism. This includes the gross use of language. And 2. where language is itself primary and ideas subservient to language. This is the field of letters, whence the prevalence of fiction and the preeminence of poetry in this division.
>
> These two major uses of language complement each other—or should in a well adjusted intelligence.

Three things are worth pointing out here. First of all, Williams is obviously reacting to something, counterattacking, defining himself and his position over against those he takes to be his opponents. In this collection these are called "Science and Philosophy," usually in capitals, almost always together (as if they constituted a partnership or corporation), and almost always as a kind of personification—not "scientists and philosophers," but "Science and Philosophy."

Second, Williams is here making a case for what we might call a nonreferential theory of language in "the field of letters." In the opposition as he outlines it, the language of journalism, science, philosophy, etc. is constantly pointing or referring to a content exterior to itself, and the words of this kind of writing are "secondary to the burden of ideas" or information. The word "tree" in a learned treatise or a newspaper article doesn't draw our attention to itself but to an image of one of those wooden things outside the window, with leaves stuck all over it. The words themselves tend to disappear from the page or our awareness of it, leaving only the images to which they refer. And the more accurate or "realistic" this kind of writing tends to be, the more transparent it is, the more the words tend to disappear, to become unreal because unexperienced.

> If words are real, not symbols, then the depiction of reality, realism, plain writing, is a denial of their actuality since the thing depicted, as in "impressionism," *is* the objective and the words are put back into their wornout usage as unreal (*i.e.,* symbols for the "reality" which is something else, the object depicted).

Instead, Williams insists that in letters "the language is itself primary" and ideas subservient to it. This kind of language insists on itself as real, it claims our attention with distortions of conventional syntax and grammar, with puns and repetition. (No wonder Joyce and Stein had such an attraction for him.)

> In Surrealism the distortion of the emotion, the object, the condition, makes the words (the true material of writing) real again.

But wouldn't this kind of writing give us an empty verbalism, words that don't refer to any concrete experience that we can know through our bodily senses? Isn't this a plea for a sort of art-for-art's-sake, bereft of ideas? If you've read many of Williams's poems you may be wondering how the question could even be raised. His work is so concrete, so sensuously immediate. If, as Wallace Stevens said, "the greatest poverty is not to live in a physical world," then Williams is one of the richest poets we've ever had, and a great part of that richness inheres in the way the language of his poems insists on itself *as* language even while it enacts experiences with a refreshing vividness. We experience his words sensorily because they focus our awareness on themselves as words even as they are accurately tuned to the facts they present.

Of course Williams is in one sense beating a dead horse. In attacking language which is "secondary to ideas" he is condemning what is called the *popular* notion of the referential theory of meaning. No philosopher of language worth bothering about holds to such a simplistic notion of the referential theory. Yet the popular notion is worth attacking precisely because it is popular. At the time Williams was writing these notes, between 1928 and 1930, many of those who read poetry were reading it (as people still do today) as if poets used language only discursively, the way scientists, philosophers and journalists do. And, not being able to "get anything out of it" that way, they were rejecting it. As they still do. Or, as they still do, they read it passively, as if it contained only a discursive component, coming away only with quotable bits of "wisdom"—Polonius' speeches, for instance.

(Polonius' creator, incidentally, is Williams's ultimate paradigm for an artist who uses language dramatically rather than—or as well as—discursively. Shakespeare's speeches enact experiences, if we read them actively. Each speech *is* an act. It's of course possible to read him passively, as if his plays were merely discourses on prudence, or jealousy, or revenge, or politics. But that is to starve ourselves at a great feast, to turn away from a great opportunity for self-discovery and -creation. Williams's version of Shakespeare may strike us at times as "William Carlos Shakespeare"—at one point he calls Shakespeare "My Grandfather." But that seems right to me. We read these notes primarily for what they tell us about Williams and his work.)

Finally, the language of the passages just quoted seems, especially for a condemnation of the scientific-philosophical use of language, to be itself curiously "philosophical." Much of Williams's language throughout *The Embodiment of Knowledge* has this quasi-philosophical ring. He is seeking here to communicate, to inform, yet he'd said earlier, in *Kora*, "Talk is servile that is set to inform." (*Imaginations*, 17) We could dismiss the whole question with the glib diagnosis that Williams is too obtuse to realize that he is here committing the very "sin" for which he damns others. Yet he says quite explicitly that the two functions of language "complement each other—or should in a well adjusted intelligence."

In order to understand (and appreciate) what appears to be a contradiction here, it's best to look at the form or apparent formlessness of this whole collection of notes. One of the implicit metaphors that controls and shapes these fragments is that of boundaries crossed, enclosures escaped from, especially the enclosing walls of the academy which, in Williams's conception, impede growth and development. The classics, for instance, *enthrall* us while they simultaneously inspire us to *break out*. (It was never any wonder to me that I sought to enrich my graduate education by taking special seminars at Boston Garden with Bill Russell.) On his very first page Williams points out that the young, "finding no 'purpose' in study . . . quite correctly conclude that a life of action outside of academic walls is preferable to a continued purposeless amassing of data within." This "amassing of data" is a miser's occupation, as if knowledge were a quantity of material to be possessed, and possessed permanently, as a farmer believes his field to be his forever. A little later Williams complains self-mockingly,

My depressed and discouraged friends look at me with curious eyes. It is, I say to myself, the century. Most have cash . . . Why am I as I am? Understanding may be lack of wit. Of what use is my understanding and what is it I have come to in the face of the world? This very note I happen to be writing at a cross street where once, in a field, I was seized by the throat, knocked down and trampled by an angry farmer, dead now, for running in and trampling his wheat . . .

Conversation has come to be impossible save among specialists in a certain pen, between the lists no language reaches.

The self-pity is at least partly ironic. Williams, with his "crazy" notions of the nature of knowledge and the non-referential language of poetry, has come to nothing. What has his own understanding brought him? Yet, he writes his complaint at a street corner which *once* was a field possessed by a certain bad-tempered farmer. The farmer thought the field his own, yet both the field and the farmer are gone and Williams remains, to write his note, in which both field and farmer are embodied. And though Williams himself is gone too now, his note remains, and preserves himself, the field and the farmer for our interaction in a way more fruitful than they would ever have been if these boundaries had never been crossed.

And can we imagine what conversation would be possible between a "trespasser" like Williams and the "possessor" of a field—even a field of knowledge? With an inhuman specialization of knowledge into discrete fields conversation is possible only between "specialists in a certain pen." Is that a writing implement or an enclosure for animals? Are they dogs in a manger?

Some fifteen pages after his anecdote about the angry farmer Williams comments, "Charming, loveable, and especially able and devoted men, one cannot speak to violently, especially uninformedly—in their fields—though one may, against the law—walk across them without getting a load of buckshot." In this collection Williams is trespassing into those areas we usually think of as belonging to scholars, academicians, educators, philosophers and scientists, and so attempts to speak a language appropriate to these fields. The two kinds of language, the poetic and the discursive, "complement each other—or should in a well adjusted intelligence." And his motivation for this trespass is truly humane (although no one will deny the defensive component in it). He doesn't come to steal or to conquer, but to liberate, to liberate scholars, students, himself and us. In criticizing scholars he enters their field and demands that when they criticize him or any other poet they enter his field, to find the knowledge that's embodied there and how it can be

nourishingly assimilated, embodied. In crossing these bound-
aries and demanding that they be crossed he asserts—in ac-
tion—their permeability. By his action he makes clear that
the "fields" are not characterized as static areas but as pro-
cesses. And it's further fitting that the collection itself takes
the form of notes in progress or process.

The typescript of these notes, as I found it in the Beinecke
Library at Yale (where a massive amount of Williams manu-
script material is stored), consists of one hundred twenty-
seven numbered, legal-size pages arbitrarily separated into
three "volumes" covered in legal-size cardboard and stapled
together. Scattered throughout these sheets are five "index"
pages which, taken together, form a (not entirely accurate)
table of contents. The script also contains two title pages
indicating that Williams had settled on *The Embodiment of
Knowledge* as his final title, together with the subtitles
which I've used in this edition. He also notes that the collec-
tion has "no arrangement—but a thorough indexing and
revision of each part." The last "volume" of the script con-
tains, after the final numbered, legal-size page, three sheets
typed by himself on his own machine (the rest of the script
was obviously prepared by a professional typist) which
contains three epigraphs and a dedication, followed by a
short essay to which I've given the title "The Pluralism of
Experience." I've allowed the epigraphs and dedication to
stand where they occur in the typescript, but I've also re-
produced them in the front matter of this edition.

The last five "Philosophical Essays" never formed part of
the original typescript of *The Embodiment of Knowledge*,
and I've placed them in a distinct section of their own in
this edition. They are included here as a somewhat more
consecutive articulation of many of the concerns Williams
takes up in *The Embodiment*. Both their style and the phys-
ical appearance of the typescript indicate that they were
written much earlier than the bulk of this collection, most
likely during the second decade of this century. They have
the charm of a young man's attempts to ground his thought

in philosophical terms, and in a form canonized by time. They sound at times like distant cousins of Plato's dialogues, but they appear to be closer in tone and style to a model at once more familiar and more "respectable" to Williams and his contemporaries, especially his older contemporaries— John Galsworthy's "Vague Thoughts on Art," which Williams's friend Alfred Stieglitz reprinted in his magazine *Camera Work* in the early teens.

Aside from the provocative nature of many of the statements Williams makes in these pages, this collection has value for the light it throws on Williams's central work, his poems, his prose, and those collections of prose-and-poetry —the work that has made him a major figure in the literature of our time. The collection seems to me more valuable for the questions it raises by its very "unfinished" quality than it might have been if he had "polished" it. Answers tend to close things off, questions to open things up. Keeping this value in mind I've tried to keep editorial changes to a minimum. I've left the pieces and fragments in their original order, only indicating more clearly than the original typescript where one piece ends and the next begins. I've silently regularized spelling, punctuation and capitalization, because the publisher and I agreed that the primary value of the collection lies in the statements it makes, not in its mechanical appearance. Williams obviously did not proofread the typescript with any great care, and it would be foolish either to preserve the casual and possibly confusing errors of his typist or to clutter up the page with a lot of carats, superscript numbers or other marginal editor's tracks. Where it seemed to me absolutely necessary, to prevent confusion, I've supplied a missing word in square brackets. In some cases I've supplied missing titles in square brackets, for the reader's convenience, so that he might refer to a piece by some handle less awkward than "that essay beginning on page 44." Interested readers will find, following the text, a section of notes in which I've commented on the text, supplied possible alternate readings for an extremely tangled passage in the script, or supplied the original reading for a passage I've emended. Especially I've wanted to preserve the original flavor of a notebook in which Williams, as he says in his *Autobiography*, "practiced the eternally rewarding game of scribbling," often "thinking out loud" on his typewriter or even with a pencil on his prescription blanks. In these notes he sometimes starts out in one direction, breaks off, backs up, repeats the beginning of an incomplete sentence, and then pushes on. In that procedure we can see him in the act of discovering what he knows, and proving in action that knowledge is a process of discovery and self-making. Contradictions are of course part of that process, and I've made no attempt to "correct" Williams's inconsistencies.

Finally, it seems to me that the collection has value, not only for the way it anticipates current positions in poetry and art, and even in that "opposition" against which Williams identified and realized himself (science and philosophy), but for the way in which it establishes him as a member of that sanest line of development in our history, those thinkers and artists who insist on the *integrity* of the human organism—thought *and* feeling, sense *and* intellection, mind *and* body. Williams aligns himself against both those who have sought to *transcend* the body or the physical for the sake of some spiritual or intellectual ideal, ("The world was made to eat, not leave," he says in *In the American Grain*, "that the spirit be full, not empty.") and against those, like Benjamin Franklin, who have sought to utilize knowledge in a project toward a notion of "perfection" which is actually inhuman. Knowledge-as-power, whether we think we possess it or only strive for it, is an addictive drug, desensitizing us to our own experience, to the rich ways in which our ignorance qualifies our knowing, and especially to our commonality as men and women. These notes, *The Embodiment of Knowledge*, help us to see how Williams, in his major works, takes his place in a line of development that goes back at least as far as Herakleitos, who also knew that "To take thought thickens the blood around the heart."

Berkeley, California   R. L.
July, 1973

The Embodiment of Knowledge

(first writing)
These are the Words

no arrangement—but a thorough indexing
and revision of each part.

"It has always been so in history, that
an entire generation has owed its outward
freedom to the inner freedom of one
individual."

My country, right or wrong.

"The book as a whole is a whole."

TO MY BOYS—
Wishing them luck

I'd like this to be printed as it is, faults and all. But don't waste
too much time on it, if you feel inclined to spend any time on
it at all.

It is intended to go along *with a life* and to be in no
sense its objective.

[signed] W.C. Williams

The Beginnings of an American Education

TODAY the underlying "fault" in all colleges is described in the phrase "the more you learn the less you know," a true description of the mind before it has reached clarity. It is the state in which the young are today generally bogged. The beginning of its resolution is in the understanding that it is a well-recognized condition in all preliminary approaches to knowledge. It is the cause of the failure of the young to wish to "finish the prescribed course," the disgust with academic material of all sorts. Finding no "purpose" in study they quite correctly conclude that a life of action outside of academic walls is preferable to continued purposeless amassing of data within, which, unless clarified, are an impediment to the intelligence rather than an aid.

The fault of "youth" lies, then, not in youth at all but with those to whom it has been asked to look: to its elders, the leaders, the professors who, when they are honest, acknowledge that they really know next to nothing at all.

The causes are to begin with, a lack of end, of purpose among us all. We have no longer the college with "God" at the head, the old theological head which in pattern is not only the type of the past but must be the type of the future also. Except that it can no longer be *that* figurehead which accomplishes the organization. Without disrespect to the faiths of others, the purpose of the present-day school can no longer be "God" in the diminished sense in which we know the old conception today. It must be newer, firmer, more inclusive, more flexible—or not at all—for new minds.

But the type, the school with a head, must prevail, the old academy was right in its organization, only its old head, the

3

particular old purpose must be replaced by a more resourceful, a more liberal, a more fertile breadth of purpose.

What that may be—whatever that may be—it must *be* or there is, indeed, an end to learning.

So it must be said, for the correction of the young, that learning remains desirable, unnicked by those who leave it behind, even with perfect rightness. The desire for and the desirability of knowledge remains there—unattainable because of a lack of definition on the part of those who would lead. It is *their* defect. Youth is right when it attacks those who would lead it and have lost the direction. When we must go by instinct, failing leadership, trust youth. But that does not mean that leadership, if it could be found, is not better. It is the most desirable thing youth should expect out of its elders. It is lacking today for lack of sight ahead.

Specifically it is not the purpose of colleges just to teach the steps to a "profession," to make itself into a mechanical master to apprentices in rather cultured trades. Its purpose should be to lead the mind to heights of understanding. Meanwhile, while waiting for that, it must also be what it can be. So one goes there for what he gets as to a five and ten cent store, precisely. It is the way to use a modern college, lacking other design.

Various methods have been sought to have the mind come out of this dilemma. Most have sought to ease the overloaded and repetitious curricula, from kindergarten up, by the synthetic method, by squeezing the matters for study up into small parcels, by simplification, by getting to the "essentials" in each subject thus to escape the perfectly futile objective of becoming really a master in everything. What an end that is, really! They must think children are stupid.

The only result achieved by that hurrying method is to have children learn nothing at all, or to learn of that to which they do pay any attention, just a bare smattering. The intelligent child resents this and does, as might be expected, as little as he can of anything—which carries the theory of his elders just a little further than intended. He doesn't give a damn for sloppy methods and cannot respect them. He is a child and can be trusted not to lie to himself—unless he prove a "good student." That is the reason for the indifference of the child toward school in most cases. He is right in his indifference under such methods.

The child knows he is not learning. He knows he is not getting at things thoroughly. He knows why he prefers the coaching of the football mentor to that of the history teacher. The first is real, the last is a lie. It is cheap, shabby stuff he learns mostly in classes. But he also knows a poor coach from a good one, and he will after all respect and follow an honest teacher of history—even when he hates history.

It is not in a gluing together of bits of knowledge that a child reaches understanding. School is a waste, a harmful waste under such a system—except to the alert and resourceful child, and only to the alert child, who circumvents the harm by use of his own mind. That virtue of deception, of double-crossing the teacher from within, is the only thing that saves the child's mind at all. He knows he must "get" the work to "pass," but he knows deeper still, that it is the bunk, and that he only needs to get enough *to* pass. By this method he rescues his intelligence, fortunately for him and for us all.

It is a pity that school has come to mean this battle of wits between alert children and the sluggards who have captured him in the name of learning when he was too young to protect himself—save by deception. It is the reason that many distinguished minds develop only after the incubus of school has slid behind them. It is almost a sign of intelligence when a boy looks at his high school work with an ironical indifference—but it is a state of mind that is dangerous and should not be accepted as final. It is also a burden which children should not be expected to carry unassisted.

Surely it cannot be escaped that the true solution of the

difficulties does not lie with synthesis but with a reawakening of the classical method of analysis—a light, a bolt even, through the chaotic murk of information, the discovery of an end to learning—something toward which the child from *any* direction may strive. It is this that must be sought.

Data should be present in activities which, in particular, have newly organized their material, such as, let us say, in poetry. How better than in poetry, that has undergone a revolution in its conceptions within twenty-five years. For it has always been to poetry that the world has turned in the past for light. At least this would be more than the hints to which practical philosophy and science have sometimes resorted. From the particular, it may be that with care—from the particular and sensitive field of the artist—certain ways may be found for the elucidation of knowledge in the general field—especially in the art of poetry, since education is accomplished almost entirely by the use of words, and words have all their contours best defined in poetry—as always.

To words and their significance—which is the special field of the poet—the educationalist must turn willy-nilly in the end. And the modern poet has been using his whole thought upon these for a quarter of a century at least, and besides it is a field which I know.

Knowledge started with the "word," it might do far worse than to go back to the beginning—with the addition of the cleansing of the "word," which is the work poets have in hand.

The implications are partial and tentative. The work is not to champion a cause, but to seek to assist the young as I may be able. Whatever may be said is not given dogmatically but with the desire to have it read by others and if found suitable for attention—to be valued as it may be valued. For I am sure that if it is not sufficiently interesting to be read by the young (not everybody, of course) it lacks pith.

We are in that stage: "the more you study the less you

know"; which is perfectly true—unless you go through—to what?—to a stillness, to that basis on which the modern excellence of the best new poetry is founded.

John Dewey and others appear to look for a solution to the problem of education in psychology and sociology—in philosophy then. They might do worse than to seek it in poetry. It is the poetic conception (see Einstein's reported statement—among others) of the universe that is the correct one. Its forms are best seen in the poetic form of an age. Philosophy could not be better occupied than in translating them to its idioms.

Not that poetry cannot learn from philosophy, but the proof of this might well be offered us out of the wisdom of our seers by reversing the courtesy—or necessity, as it may be. And, let them be less slow, as seems apparent, in following the poetry that is vulgarly unaccepted about them and not turn with the unthinking to the poetry of an age which is bankrupt much by their own thought.

If the modern poet, beset with the stupidity of fire-breathing propagandists, who see nothing to observe but cling to what "I like"—may he not turn to thinking men for support. And why may not the thinker himself learn, perhaps, in the poetic application of thought, something to think about.

A writer is a person whose best is released in the accomplishment of writing—perhaps it is a good variant to say—in the act of writing. He does not necessarily think these things—he does not, that is, think them out and then write them down: he writes and the best of him, in spite even of his thought, will appear on the page even to his surprise, unrecognized or even sometimes against his will, by proper use of words.

Example of Boy Beginning His "Education"

FROM THIS he learns, not what he is taught—things which are indifferent to him—but certain things which are taken over into the general field of learning (give him a habit of mind) and may be developed in this way. Take as example: the boy, seventeen, having resided in France for a year, returns to school to finish his course, and takes the final year's work in that language. The teacher is a young woman who does not know the language save from the classroom stand. She has succeeded another teacher whose methods differ from her own. The class consists of eight boys and girls. The one person in the class who knows French is the boy mentioned, he is contemptuous of the teacher's accent and the other pupils' general ignorance and *so* ignores the particular instruction which unreasonably is being detailed —catchwords and idiomatic phrases which a Frenchman *might* not know and yet be able to speak the language perfectly. And yet on this basis the child who has not memorized what the teacher has given him receives a bad mark in French, and she who has the daily drill by heart is rewarded. He cannot overcome this mark which is unfair, an inaccurate index of knowledge and relates only to a particular teacher's general ineptitude. The boy in question is perfectly right in his contempt for the teacher and the pupils alike, who cleverly band together immediately after a class to compare notes and get by rote the things *that* teacher wants them to know and which they know she will ask in tests.

Interviewed afterward she shows the marks, they range from 85 to 60. Those that have been in my class from the first have the highest marks—because they know my system. Or, the boy has an exceptional background, his vocabulary is above the average, he knows his grammar, he is responsive in class *but* he only received a 60 on his test. In what class of questions did he fail? Oh, just small things, a matter of pure memory (the particular things which he should have conned from his notebook which was not kept up to date.) This is the same *position* of intelligence.

This seems to be the characteristic American *position* of the intelligence—the pioneer turn of mind—the individual superior to authority. No, external to it, [authority, as] connotated by our history, [our] temperament—the one [position] profitably to be observed.

No attempt is made to correlate [the chapters to follow] except insofar as to relate them back to the original indirect *position*, outside of "learning." The European medieval aspiration toward a peak, aristocratic striving: the American toward a useful body of knowledge made to serve the individual who is *primary*.

The Beginnings of an American Education

Chapter 2. The Address Toward Collegiate Study. The New in Art.

> "Many of them had better have been clerks in an office."
>
> Dimnet.

AN ART STUDENT has difficulty in *knowing*, in fact, it is the major and final lesson that as a student he has to learn, that when he has mastered something that has been done in the past, and that his teachers have worked mightily to demonstrate to him, he has learned nothing but that which is reprehensible in an artist, of no use to him, in fact nothing less than a barrier which he must surmount if ever he is to do anything that can be called serious work.

This is true of all studies, but it is their stigma that the old forms mean little in their quasi-moribund composition.

But in art, which is the quintessence of knowledge, the category most responsive to living conditions, the most sensitive to the damages caused by lumber of all sorts, which ruin its accuracy, it is fatal.

A painter like Cézanne or Titian, or a statue as good as some by Phidias, is a complete triumph to the learned, and worth nothing whatever.

[*Shakespeare*]

November 17, 1929.

Why was not Shakespeare, the "entertainer," better known in his own day and his name celebrated so that the details of his life and his person should have come down to us? Why, where so famous a work was done, did so little fame impress his contemporaries? Simply, he did not exist for them. He lived only in his plays. This obvious truth has led the facile imagination to believe that he did not exist at all, childishly too easy an explanation, which misses completely the great critical opportunity in face of the work itself—and its meaning which is the sole object of present day studies.

Shakespeare's work is all words. The time was a time of deeds. Anyone in such a time who was just a player, good witty fellow though he may be, will not be remembered for his life and Shakespeare was not.

It is the value of words that is the problem involved. Man the speaking animal. Man, then at his highest pitch. Yes or No? Words are deeds? Or what is to be said? Shakespeare's words have turned out great actors.

By this the great interest in Shakespeare becomes the human one. Men in all, seeing, living—under the cloud of action. And what is their destiny? Or what does action after all accomplish comparable to words, to speech, to expression. To poetry. To all art, in short. To cathedrals even—for there, though it were a Blanche at the back of it, the architects drew and imagined the plans and the silent crowds gave meat to the imagination through which to work. What

11

is man and why does he speak and what does he say? This is the unprecedented Shakespeare who spreads in reputation as time passes and does *not* sink back upon a past deed— though in his day he was just so much talk.

Shakespeare's first characteristic is that all his writing is immediately related to an act, in contradistinction to the purveyances of scholards whose words are related to acts, if at all, only intermediately through thought.

Shakespeare is unique in this, his plays are his life to such an extent that they have submerged, exchanged currents with it, to such an extent that he, as the character of a writer, has ceased to exist. Nowhere else in literature has this occurred. Not once, throughout a lifetime, has Shakespeare the writer appeared outside the deed.

His philosophy is obvious and simple, it is his writing. Writing, real in a real world where deeds are futile but imperative but the reality of man is an imaginative speech: Hamlet, himself the protagonist of the writer both male and female: man sunk in a world of transparent accordances— that succeed like scenes and acts to no end—save himself.

The implications, pregnancies, consequent thereto, the relevancies, the irrelevancies and particularly the light it casts on certain phases of scholarship—are worth an indulgence.

—and scholarly talk of it—that is not even in the category of that which it seeks to discuss, just so much excrement.

— — — — — — — — — —

I suppose *Hamlet* was truer of him—fond of making farewell speeches, than any of the other characters—that's why he liked it best. The "mystery" of Hamlet is not in *Hamlet* but in all the plays and their writer—in all players and in all writers—in all deeds and in all failures to come to a deed —and yet the deed of speeches in which man is most real.

"Realism" has one inevitable catch in it: it is not suscepti-ble to writing, to being written as a transcription of events or even facts (a thing philosophy has never dared envisage under penalty of eschewing writing altogether). To tran-scribe the real creates, by the same act, an unreality, some-thing besides the real which is its transcription, since the writing is one thing, what it transcribes another, the writing a fiction, necessarily and always so.

The only real in writing is writing itself. This is a gift or certain genius barred to scholarship—open to the blind, per-haps, and to the imprisoned.

For Shakespeare to have put down his thoughts, his life, in writing would have been realism, an unreality for him to have cogitated on the state of the times and his soul and to have so retailed them for purchase to the attention—might have proved an amusing verification of the similarity of all times and an extenuation of the faults of this, but it would not have made Shakespeare living today. But to have writ-ten a hundred characters is *himself*, true, actual. He could not distinguish between the thinker and the doer. He could not himself, a sham, appear.

And scholars may analyze and twist and squirm, annotate and compare, wash down, sift and refine, reject and acclaim but they will never achieve *that*, for it is outside the cate-gory of their investigations.

It is in itself a criticism of their function, standing beyond them:—native woodnotes wild. It is pure writing that can't get away from itself to be thought. Thought is not writing, to write betrays both writing and itself. So Shakespeare is disclosed fixed in a world, as actual as a tree.

Thought would be more "himself," what he thinks, and so permit a subversion he never countenanced.

Better for scholarship, to take a modern turn and reject Shakespeare as a thinker—it at least cleans the attention. But a condition is by this left unguarded. If Shakespeare is a second-rate dispenser of philosophies in whose works profundities of "thought" are not to be discovered, how shall his genius be rated?

Why is the work itself, obvious though unperceived. His excellence is his fault. He will be rated as a writer.

—the futility of deeds, and that man is real only as an imaginative speech.

—and the more keen, the more immanent the perception, practice, realization of this *in the work*, the more actual the writing. In Shakespeare's case a physiologic inevitability, the constitution of his genius itself.

Shakespeare's weakness in thought is his peculiar strength: he is not divorced by thought from a persistent actuality. His rejection, inevitable by philosophy and scholars, is his philosophic strength. He stands outside the thought which encloses his work not in "thoughts" their trouble. He is not a dealer in abstractions using a play as a subterfuge, words, writing as a means. But the writing is all and only.

He belongs to anyone, for this, who can read him—but particularly *not* to scholarship and scholars.

October 30, 1929.

I will draw a picture of Shakespeare as I conceive him to have been, an inevitable prophet of the world as it is coming to be today. It is of no consequence whatever that he may be conceived otherwise, it will not be unproven that my conception is anything but appropriate to his plays. I conceive him so for my purpose.

Were it not so he would never have begun with the light, smart, somewhat clumsy comedies—of little meat and no premeditation—lit by small flashes in certain lines but essentially good theatre and that is all; then grow, grow into the thing and over a lifetime produce the cloth of a life—his own—with profounder artistry (not thought) succeeding each success. Shakespeare is nowhere thought, he is all play, all *the* play. It is real, unique, impossible unalterable, fast.

Thought occurs nowhere in Shakespeare as such. It is his distinctive quality that gives the unapparent hardness, the actuality that has projected it forward and will and must continue to do so. It is parcel with *a* life. (The same as in Lenin.) The plays are pure biography and biography of an illiterate man, who could not use words for things. The mind is primitive, only such words he used as stood for action. They were not used as logic, for words as a learned man uses them to transmit abstract ideas. They were a switchboard for things and people's growth and movements, in reverse. The actions pressed the keys and recorded them on the page.

Shakespeare the country boy of genius, ambition, abundant fancy and no learning at all, frail perhaps, not at least focused in the center of his belly nor in the arms: was drawn to London in a time—or forced there—for where else could he go with a taste for pleasures of the imagination in that time. Marlowe was twenty years old, talk was free. An actor's life and vocabulary. Shakespeare took the print, it became fixed. But he had, unknown to him, or any of them, what the city gallant and the scholar were divorced from, a country man's sense of the fastness of the world of things, the moods of natural phenomena.

Eyes, ears, a tongue, words and a convivial spirit soaked in a world seething of deeds and their repercussions in minds at the center, London, with a certain country shrewdness for success—and a saving ignorance of the futility of both science and philosophy, then waking, gave him a peculiar advantage. He was stopped but freed, by the stop impelled even to contort his wit doubly hard and to be twice real to achieve reality and compete with scholars who lose as they gain. It is this which gave his work brilliance and permanence.

He did not invent story or form, he did invent reality in the words which stemmed back directly to things, to the ground, to his own simplicity, directness, and after all emptiness.

October 29, 1929.

In Shakespeare there was a certain stopped condition of mind, English and rural, which permitted him infinite elaboration and variety inside the confinement. (Greek genius, as a whole, had the same incentive, a rigid enclosure of physical actuality penetrated only by touches of inspiration from Egypt, Mesopotamia, India or as it might be. Shakespeare in like manner was touched by the keen minds, like nations, about him with which he was not really in connection half as much as he was in physical contact with the bare actualities of his difficult life.) He seems not to have been even attracted beyond a certain style, a rigidity of imagination, a paucity in one direction, that of form, which with tremendous force really compelled a human elaboration—natural to a lower social status—which offered him his only opportunity.

This does not have to do with the original impetus to art at all and to the balance and varieties of his genius—but it is confirmed by the pagan philosophy, his unchristian material and bare references—it was his unique life.

When the mind is one piece the elaboration of details becomes clear and infinite—like a category—such as science, etc. It goes on into an infinite series—only in confusion is there blurring. In Shakespeare the limpid, untroubled, unimagined variant is proof of an amazing fixity.

The Modern Primer

WHY NOT write sonnets? Because, unless the idea implied in the configuration can be de-formed it has not been *used* but copied. *All* sonnets mean the same thing because it is the configuration of the words that is the major significance. Because it is a configuration (the sonnet) whose meaning supercedes any idea that may be crammed into it. It is not an invention but anchors beyond the will—does not liberate the intelligence but stultifies it—and by its cleverness, apt use stultifies it the more by making pleasurable that which should be removed.

What is the meaning of Gertrude Stein's work? Language being made up of words, the spaces between words and their configurations, Gertrude Stein's work means that these materials are real and must be understood, in letters, to supercede in themselves all ideas, facts, movements which they may under other circumstances be asked to signify. Having removed the burdensome configurations of grammar and rhythm from her prose, Gertrude Stein seems now to have gone as far as possible in her work. It is a valuable record. It permanently states that writing to be of value to the intelligence is not made up of ideas, emotions, data, but of words in configurations fresh to our senses.

Is James Joyce's recent work a progression or a regression as related to *Ulysses?* Why? Joyce's work in "Work in Progress" is the inevitable outcome of processes which he first realized in *Ulysses.* He has attacked the words themselves as the materials of letters—whereas Gertrude Stein has dealt mostly with their configurations—realizing that the intelligence is at a stop in them (as exemplified by the emotional and intellectual limits any one language puts upon the group using it—the stultification implied in the word "patriotism"). Thus his new work is infinitely superior to that in *Ulysses*. And Joyce has used his creation far more effectively than has Stein, developing it into organic creations of new rhythmical and intellectual creations whereas Stein's work has become badly repetitious of late.

That may be true (of these writers) but in taking up individual pieces of their work, can they be understood and enjoyed? And is that not after all the true test of excellence in letters? Parts of Stein's work, and certain shorter pieces are enjoyable in a unique manner, the mind being liberated to function in a new way—a pure pleasure in letters. But some of her work seems incomprehensible and repetitious, if not boring. Stein needs editing, needs it badly. But it is a new field. A rule worth following being not to enjoy what cannot be understood—reject it as second grade.

What influence, if any, have these two writers had on others? Their influence has been active in many of the younger writers not by directly forming their style but by making certain modes of writing, now demoded, impossible to them. This is the most beneficent of influence possible, akin to the deeply underlying principles in all branches of knowledge which do not appear on the surface, but lie at the base of their sincerity and effectiveness. If words are real and are realized to be the material of letters, false reliance on emotion and idea will be whittled away. Thus all the new writing (tho' not necessarily derived or influenced by Stein or Joyce) will be found to be sharper, harder in detail, more faceted—at its best. Much of Hemingway's work is based on the qualities, the word qualities Stein has separated out in a pure form.

Do the French sur-realists owe anything to Gertrude Stein's work? Yes, assuredly. For if words are real, not symbols, then the depiction of reality, realism, plain writing, is a denial of their actuality since the thing depicted, as in "impressionism," *is* the objective and the words are put back into their wornout usage as unreal (*i.e.*, symbols for the "reality" which is something else, the object depicted). But in sur-realism the distortion of the emotion, the object, the condition, makes the words (the true material of writing) real again. Out of them (real) the illusions of sur-realism (unreal) are created.

What about the new theories advocated in the last *transition*. What about Eugene Jolas' new theories in the last *transition*, the new mythology? Is it a valid objective for writing? Yes, but not for the reasons which Jolas appears to put forward. In themselves the tenets of a new mythology would be as useless as the old. But in the making of them words would again be offered a broad sweep through which to assert their power. They would or might be composed as real objects to mould the psyche of peoples over again, thus reasserting their own powerful   and by blasting away the stultifying association with the old mythology which has denied them their dynamic potentialities by fixing them in meanings which prostitute the intelligence.

But by breaking up formulas would we not be merely losing sight of fixed truths which we need for our continued intellectual existence, would we not be reverting to nonsense without any compensatory gain—even were it possible to break up language to that extent? No. Language is the key to the mind's escape from bondage to the past. There are no "truths" that can be fixed in language. It is by the breakup of the language that the truth can be seen to exist and that it becomes operative again. Such reasoning as Spengler's depends on the fixities of language which it is the purpose of such writers as Joyce and Stein—fail tho' they may in detail—to blast. In language lodge the prejudices, the compulsions by which stupidity and ineptitude rule intelligences superior to their own.

What is the province of letters? The province of letters is that realm of the intelligence in which words and their configurations are real and all ideas and facts with which they deal are secondary. It is the complement of all other realms of the intelligence which use language as secondary to the reality of their own materials—such as science, philosophy, history, religion, the legislative field. Hence in letters the prevalence of fiction and the predominance of poetry.

What is its function? Its function is to re-enkindle language, to break it away from its enforcements, its prostitutions under all other categories. For language that is used as a means to an end foreign to itself is language used as an expedient—something that cannot be scientifically or philosophically sanctioned—impurely. This is "symbolism." It is a union of expediency which tends to crumble apart as the words shift in meaning or become dead. Thus Jefferson said, Liberty to be preserved requires a revolution every twenty years. By taking language as real and employing it with a full breadth and sweep, letters frees it from encroachments and makes it operative again. Lewis Carroll was an important creator in their abstract field. Smollett knew something of this service.

French Painting

(Its Importance, a Definition, and the Influence Upon Modern Writing Traceable to It)

THERE IS a progressive excellence moving through the periods marked each by an ism in the last hundred years of French painting. It is technical and its influence is traceable there as well as in the other arts. It is a longer phase than the generational modalities of it which attract periodic attention.

It is, in paint, an effect of this plain problem: How shall the multiplicity of a natural object, impossible to detail or completely encircle, be presented by pigment on canvas. Plainly it is not to trace it as it stands for that intelligence is impossible, repetitious and uncalled for. (It is, in effect, an analysis, first, of the scene, followed by technical virtuosity.) It is to represent some phase of this object that the schools point. Each pose caught being a success.

Realizing this, the exhilarating resourcefulness and fertility of the French is shown, but being part of a general problem, there is (beyond that) a liberalizing implication to it which releases from the particular train—train of the French thing of the moment, which seduces artisans in the same craft elsewhere.

It is a fundamental technical problem. It is faced when a tree is to be put on canvas. (Shall it be one etched leaf in the foreground? a contour of massed branches, a color— or what?)

Facing it, realizing that it is pigment on a surface, French painting went as far as Braque, it became a surface of paint and that is what it represented. It went to this extreme to free itself of misconceptions as to its function, after that and before that, what? for that was its simplest and most extreme, most sanitary phase. (It remains the pivot for an appraisal of its continued activity.)

For this is the flat of it: all painting is representation and cannot be anything else. This must be stated in order to clear the looseness of some thought concerning it and to understand it properly. It was a mistake to say, as it was said twenty years ago, that the object of modern painting was to escape representation. Not so. (It was to escape triteness, the stupidity of a loose verisimilitude—to trace a scene and thus to confuse paint values with natural objects.)

It *is* to represent nature. The only problem being: what shall we represent and how? In that choice lies the whole of the artist's realm. It is evidence of the exercise of this choice that is to be judged, finally, as excellent. It is a technique along with a stress of experience (the understan ling, intelligence) that shall not at least be false thought, stale emotion and lying pretense (of delineation).

Invention (creation) being basically the mark of intelligence, selecting and rejecting its material—as it would be in an engineer that turns to the time for his opportunity.

French painting from this viewpoint escaping the cliché of the predominant ism of the moment can be highly instructive to the writer—and has been to me—being as I believe it to have been for a hundred years one of the cleanest, most alert and fecund avenues of human endeavor, a positive point of intelligent insistence from which work may depart in any direction.

The writer is to describe, to represent just as the painter must do—but what? and how?

It is the same question of words and technique in their arrangement—Stein has stressed, as Braque did paint, words. So the significance of her personal motto: A rose is a rose— which printed in a circle means two things: A rose is, to be sure, a rose. But on the other hand the words: A rose is —are words which stand for all words and are very definitely not roses—but are nevertheless subject to arrangement for effect—as are roses—and shall be, for themselves, as meaningless—or as the arrangement which is jointed upon them shall please. In this case the words are put there to represent words, the rose spoken of being left to be a rose.

Let it be noted that these two phases, writing and painting, occurred synchronously. The basis is, presumably, a common one. As thought underlies.

1. The artist "idea" is not to limit, not to constrict, but not to fly off into "universals," into vapors, either. That is what it is to be an artist with his material before him. It is to be a kind of laborer—a workman—a maker in a very plain sense—nothing vague or transcendental about it: that is the artist—at base.

2. The basis being—that one can come up through to excellence in the arts—as to an intelligent use of his life—anywhere—at any time—tho' with variations—and this is a liberal understanding of the world and an American one.

3. (last bit) It is because we confuse the narrow sense of parochialism in its limiting implication, that we fail to see the complement of the same: that the local in a full sense *is* the freeing agency to all thought, in that it is everywhere accessible to all: not in the temple, of a class, but for every place where men have eyes, brains, vigor and the desire to partake with others of that same variant in other *places* which unites us all—if we are able.

4. And how do the French do this: Strictly by following a local tradition. Their painting is a consecutive series of modulations on a craft. It has two collateral phases (1) taking from Japanese, Italian, Spanish—any craft, and being able to do so because the local permits it and (2) attracting other craftsmen in a great manner whose genius to use for themselves: Picasso, Gris—Cosmopolis be damned. Cosmopolis is where I happen to be. The virtue of Paris is not that it is a world capital of art. Facile nonsense. It is that Paris is a French city, dominated by French ideas—attracting the good to that, to that positive. None more local than the French: its vigor. It is the local that is the focus of work—

everywhere available. It *is* (the local—with myself present in it) cosmopolis, a theoretical universal which is constricting—a self-apparent denial of the universality of the very fact of art itself.

1. The painters have paid too much attention to the ism and not enough to the painting. I'm for the painting where it is, in America or elsewhere, but I'm not for morons—vigor, worth, fervor—wherever it is and don't be seduced by it save for the pleasure and the impregnating point of it—which isn't an ism—or of the moment.

2. Someone by the name of Stearns has kicked against the pricks of French painting, saying that it has seduced American painters as it has, save for a few. All right. If the rest are not witty enough to circumvent, even use, that influence —to hell with them.

French painting has been, is a living, vigorous thing. There are not enough such in thought and act in the world on that plane. As a writer I enjoyed and profited. Here's the solution.

3. As to the laying on of the pigment, of course, I know nothing—save from common observation: that there are many ways—in work that is excellent from Van Dyke through Rembrandt to Cézanne.

4. What shall be seen then in America? Nothing French surely. What is there to see? A tree—it's been painted a myriad times from the Renaissance background down to Derain.

Well, what does one see? to paint? Why the tree, of course, is the facile answer. Not at all. The tree as a tree does not exist literally, figuratively or any way you please—for the appraising eye of the artist—or any man—the tree does not exist. What does exist, and in heightened intensity for the artist is the impression created by the shape and color of an object before him in his sensual being—his whole body (not his eyes) his body, his mind, his memory, his place: himself—that is what he sees—And in America—escape it he cannot—it is an American tree.

Render that in pigment and he asserts his own existence and that of men about him—he becomes prophet and seer—in so far as he is wholly worthy to be so.

That is the significance, the penetration, the wit and power of a picture. If he can record that with (and it is always a technical problem of) mastery and material, he will be presenting a tree. To do less, to ape a French manner is to put out his eye—then surely he has not seen the tree at all. She is the appendage of someone else who has subjugated him.

Science and Philosophy

CHILDREN, at birth, used to be made blind by a venereal infection of the eyes, until we used silver nitrate in every case. But the whole world has been and is blinded now by the effects of Science and Philosophy from birth up. Science is a deceit; Philosophy a sham; these are not life, but a scum over it through which we see torturedly. But poetry is the breath of life itself. Learning—to hell with it. Yet we must know, that's all. And when we know, and do, it is poetry. The big paper figures which they carry on sticks in parades give one only a disease. Poetry alone holds that can save us.

People, that's all there is in the world—and animals and plants and Pasteur's crystals—with whom we do not think. It is nothing but a cheated existence to think, think, think. And to do, do, do is still worse: but to know is everything and includes both knowing and thinking, for it is a clarity, objects come up clear. People seem crystals. They are crystals when we do and know what we do.

But science and philosophy with all its grotesque wall paintings of half men, half women, men walking, sitting down with little feet projecting like birds' legs from the middle of their buttocks, and a wheel under their brains; these (science and philosophy) come between men and men, men and women. They are even forced between instead of being relegated to pits—as we do a roast beef, a little iron pot over the fire, a little pit to stew it in that we may eat it.

But clarity! is life. The unscummed impact of the sense and mind—servants of (How can it be named save in a moment of passion, that is why it cannot be dissected by the sheepheads). There isn't a whole man alive. The time detests it. Slowly for hundreds of years the ones above have sought to suppress the ones beneath. War is not even war. There are no men—but only pity, a desperate, dejected, defeated crowd—sometimes of almost saints. But no one has named the defeat that every soldier felt.

No clarity. It does, does it not, appeal at once when it is seen. Science. Philosophy. Hundreds of years building to keep life from its impacts. Jealousy. Hatred of each other. Defeat. To hedge life. To hold it in bounds. Guard your wife. Guard your money. Learn, but do not touch. Be a scientist but not a man. Or if a man not a scientist but in interim—escaping. "He is a great scientist—but a man." Until it has gradually come to be more and more [a] subtle film catching us all. A gross bar between [us and] life, such as a Greek slave had—we suppose. Until DEMOCRACY—has come, which is a thin, scientifically, philosophically perfect film, we can just see through enough. Flexible as collodion, as invisible as an electric sheet. Tough, universal—a magic lining between men everywhere and their desire. Even into the laws. That is why money is desired more than ever. To buy off. And they do not even know that it exists.

Courage is being managed so that it leads not where it will hit. The U. S., land of the film. Use a good toothpaste. Poetry is something else. Villon is an early type of the first man sensing the day.

Because the knife is polished they think it's sharp.

THE RICH are all liars. Kings were specimens. Can't they see it, the god damned science-philosophy blinded, not in themselves, of course, but caught in the effects of the times. Beggars they all are, and not even clever ones, like gypsies whom no one knows have a legitimate and trenchant, important, clear place in the world today. But the rich are beggars, what in the world to do but to give money to hospitals, to colleges, to laboratories, to discover the cure for beri-beri. Fine. But what do they get out of it? Humane satisfaction. What the poor wish they could steal from them. But they are really, if they knew it, stealing just that *from the poor*. From African tribes, from miserable half-castes. Brazilian Indians. London kikes.

But kings lived. Or the imagination of them does. Can't men see, not plays, in Shakespeare, but observation. Poetry. It happens, not is made. Can't they see that the decay of the monarch all through his work is one of the most important documents in existence. But. It came in big chunks. Now it is varnished down. We look through democratic varnish.

To return to anything like values and clarity, we have been forced into vulgarity. This is history. It has been driven down. Can't they see the scientific, philosophic inevitability and the—also inevitable—wrongness of the Soviet thrust to grow right. It MUST BE as it is and it has been degraded. By false direction stretching back two thousand years by the varnishers, the thinkers who have degraded and disarmed us.

Poetry then is almost all that remains high and untouched

by science and philosophy. It is akin to the lowly? But even that is not Gray's "Elegy" or "The Cotters' Saturday Night." Or John Greenleaf Whittier. The relationship is infinitely more subtle—and in fact of a different fibre. It has to do with clarity, or the whole being, that is not satisfied with lowliness, but demands to be the highest, a king—touching the world directly but is as it is—lowly—since it is surrounded by the invisible net of the liars.

And we send boys to college. But how to learn? I do not know. But in poetry there is a clew. It is this that makes that live. It is that which makes poetry indispensable to him who has lived, knows what it is to come clear and—or, there may be one or two.

June 23, 1928.

(Without Money—title—Some get it and keep it, others do not get it, others get it and let it slip.
Love:—become so damned intimate with a person you scarcely know.
The N. N: All about money and its beginning—deceptions, shoddy accompanimentative paraphernalia.

                        Sell your car
                        Rent your home
                        Obtain a position
                        Advertise in
                            the P. Daily News
Whole Milk   4 T
Water   5 oz.

Poetry

IF THEY ONLY knew what they are talking about. Not Science. Philosophy. Life. They are like a colored woman making up a patent bed inside a plate-glass window—and the silly mob outside gaping. They don't know *round* their jobs. They don't even know that what they are at is completely contained and can be limited and defined—or at least it doesn't get into their work. Everything is not being developed, it is perfect, always. The Christian Seaman's home is perfect. It is a thing in itself, sensitive and operative in its own sphere, beside Science and Philosophy. It is only stupid when you transcendentalize it, give it a future "onward and upward forever"—But if they knew half—any experienced fool does.

Then comes poetry and why shouldn't the little lovers be happy? since all love is little—the act goes dwindling off to nothing as soon as the aroma is proved. The Aragonian fire becomes small like a ring with a stone in it.

But poetry continues. Since it happens always justly, never lying, never in front of life but around it when it occurs, unlike anything else in existence: proven, just exact.

The History of a Coterie

THE MODERN versifier must not however be deceived by what I say: science may be one thing but knowledge is another. You must know. *Vers libre* be damned. It was a passing, necessary phase. To write it now is not to know. It would do good to go back to some of Ezra Pound's original don'ts for the Imagists. Work, study, try, experience, and reject. Almost everything is worthless.

4. Poetry then, and once more and finally—to the last breath.

(insert Dot bit)

6. There is nothing else for a man in the face of the world. No teaching, no friend, no wisdom. I walk alone and in silence in the city. My hero is Daniel Boone. People are less than alders.

June 23.

I am the universal husband, the only difference being they tell me and do not tell their husbands-in-law and mothers-in-the-flesh when they are about to—when I am about to be and am deceived. A real gain. On the cattle boat or anywhere.

All of it, and, that Rabelais is not "truth," (that lie)—but clarity. Clarity is the word. That is the power of it, as a whole—not the humanity, not the this, the that, but as a whole it stands outside and—is clear. A clean wind through the chaff of truth. Alive again:

33

This is what throws off poetry.

Direct vision—knowledge to action, to knowledge: Clarity is rare. Words are the fabric of poetry—but I am inclined to agree with Pound—that Joyce (and Stein) are "picking in the wrong ash can" in their recent work. It is great laboratory work. But so great is my admiration for *Ulysses* and for the artist, that I am eager to say that I feel I may be very wrong in my estimate of what he is doing now. The sheer thrust of *Ulysses* as a clarity, in the sense I mean, is far above the words themselves which he has taken now to developing.

At any rate there is a field of clear statement, clear and simple, that must run beside the fabrications of such workers. It comes of full and straight and plain statement (but not outside the words) (never) whose justice is in the meaning more than in the words. Life that flares in and fills them out like collapsed balloons. That all that is written has been lies.

One does not need to be young. Hell with that. One might know it at the brink of destruction. Yeats had tried his best to say it recently. Usually do realize it at the brink. Drowning. Life. Whole. In a desert of science-philosophy.

Eliot tried to say it in *Waste Land*—then died. But he failed. Too deceived, sold to knowledge, too frail. He could not. (He had to retire.)

It is clear. It goes through everything, from history through Eliot: He failed (beautifully—nauseously: "Sweeny and the Nightingales" being a throwing on the screen of the desire) and fell back after a gallant attack, fell back into knowledge and its ensieged—besieged citadel where it is stagnant English: which is perfectly all right save for what went before it—in his case: implications, connotations.

For Christ's sake pull your bloomers down, everybody's looking at you. You're not ten years old any more.

Reiteration: Science and Philosophy. These are provinces (necessary to explore) of my knowledge (my knowledge) which is always perfect and whole. This is the basis of criticism—Rabelais, Shakespeare.—No matter how far they go, it is always in a division which, the highest it can achieve is to reflect my completion in its segment (where each part has a definite simulacrum appearance of the whole)—which is life-exhaling poetry—the reflect that is complete and clear.

I am sick and tired of this picayune, piecemeal (all tied up), this—criticism of nice balances and picking at lines and works—valuable as it is—but. If they say to me: Well you do not know your subject. What is that? I say, Drop that. Know me. You can't? Then your knowledge is useless. When you, the acknowledged learned, have acquired a comprehension of me, revering me, giving yourself to the abandonment of all else (as you ask me to give myself to the acquirement of learning—emulate your own instructions to me in acquiring what you offer)—then, according to your own rules, begin to discuss. Your knowledge is one of the provinces I allocate to you to work in. Bring what you have prepared and make it ready so that it may be handy when I need it. That's your business. Mine is to be perfect.

Criticism is legitimately concerned [with] gauging the weight, force, significance, penetration of a work as a whole —in relation to things outside it—locating it apart from the minutiae of scholarship—the plays of Shakespeare. In fact—

Detail: What of it if I am incapable of it? Something else surrounds it. That holds me complete—and am I anything but ignorant of its effects *in petto*—But there is something else. Let them drop that and meet me in my knowledge—far more extensive than theirs: Kings have always done it.

A piece of experience—of any kind—but especially of love is meat that enriches the whole body.

On Things in General

Scholarship cannot be simplified, made available to the crowd. It will always be the function and the delight of the scholars. Realize this fully—not imagine differently: But it can be segregated in the general understanding, allotted—and not allowed to run loosely about in ungoverned stations. (It not only can but must be segregated; for how can it expect to hold a place save on an equal footing with every other thing? It must have a place beside an equal validity for other entities such as people and objects, to be able to function freely among them.) Thus, having a place from which to start, it is limited by that location. It must have a locus—which loose understanding, when it destroys that, limits the power of knowledge to operate.

But more disastrous is it for the human mind to be shadowed by something which seems to supercede it, as knowledge in the mind of "the great" seems to do, and must do if it be not subjected to rational judgment outside itself. The reverence in which knowledge is held had better be understood as an instinctive reaction to a "clarity." Thus it is not the amount that a man knows but that he has achieved a clear vision through difficulties. He has achieved what in effect is understood by a poem. The knowledge, the materia, becomes then (as it must always be to him) nothing—save by crude misconception. The actuality is the "solution." But this is in the vulgar mind, instinctive only.

Thus what is achieved is like every other clear sense, or resolution of any group of confusions. It is exactly the same, and I mean exactly, as that achieved by a peasant or a seaman —celebrated without too great acumen or penetration by Wordsworth. This is the man before whom the learned stand in awe and reverence—exactly as the vulgar (not "placed" as the peasant is) stand before the achievements of learning.

This is the same clarity achieved by love, a resolution of the personality of another and so of all personalities—

I do not do what I want to. It is that I have done always what I want to? Thus I am dissatisfied.

(Knowledge) cont. It must be seen to be what it is. It must be seen to be what it is lest the scholar himself be his own dupe—as he is most often, thinking that he is achieving values which as a fact he is losing—passing through him like the pole on which Munchausen spitted the bear by larding it—what it is. Not a universal panacea for "ignorance," not a good thing at all save for a very special purpose. And a very limited purpose (directly) unless one stand outside it and see that this purpose is exactly the same as that of a peasant of a violin maker or a husband or a horse-breeder (where all men regain the dignity of equality). That it is not the direct object of scholarship that is the but, but clarity, a clarity. And this clarity is the essence of "poetry." I use the [quotation marks] since poetry is generally known as a certain assembly of words. It is not, however, that at all. It is an effect which men skilled in the use of words put down in the words and so, when successful, succeed in evoking. But this is only a special skill. Poems are an achievement, a human achievement—though not necessarily so since the same state may be imagined as achievable by animals and plants—which the special word-skill of some man has cornered in that way. Others do it with stone, colors, etc. Love, chemistry, mathematics, astronomy, philosophy—These things lie on a par, each with the skill of anyone who goes

through his adjacent or chosen material to that clarity
which is the liberating desire of all. Even a thief has respect,
almost a murderer—because of it, and would be humanely
forgiven. Murder could be a thing so clear, so perfectly
made as to win universal acclaim.

Thus on such a basis knowledge becomes humanized or
is seen to be always human—differing only in scale from
every other human thing and not above or below it. It is
only against a nonexistent fetish that a treatise is directed
and must be. It is only against a taboo.

The Aristotelian, the Aaron, the priest of knowledge,
the select—the good, the true and the beautiful—do not exist.
The beautiful has been the first to go. Only the human
exists. Men who shut out the crowd are not fools but
maimed. Theirs has been a stupidity, not an achievement.
They may establish a bureaucracy, a priesthood, a "sacred
grove," but not without the cost of befoozlement—tho' with
the delight which all sectional solution brings—narcotization.

July 7, 1928.

Scholars, academicians—They are truly lost in the pursuit
of knowledge. To bring them back to their own true pur-
pose, of a clarity, would be at the same time to humanize
them, since knowledge is always human, only its fetish is
otherwise.

But this is the object of "the church." Very well, name it
"God"—what matter? This is where the meaning of clarity
is apparent. The church is plainly a thing, a curious approxi-
mation to a great truth. It need not bother us in any of its
forms, to study it can only lead through a maze to an outlet
where we already, without that knowledge, stand and have
always stood. The objects of such knowledge being only
to confuse, being within, by making believe one is outside,
the gist of such learning seeming to apply to the world
whereas in reality it is no more than the anatomization of—
A clarity would be to see the altogether simple thing of the

church, the colleges, as true things of strange contour like everything else, and bent like everything else upon the same end: to be clear, an end to understanding. It has the right answer to the secular colleges—call the end what they like by their history. But by a broader, humaner view we may place the image high and clear. It becomes to us a clarity, without special knowledge and alive and right in all its colors, breathing—and as it is.

1. It behooves a poet, then—a writer that is—to pay close attention to what poetry there is in the world and of what it is made lest he fall far behind and find his verse stale in the mouths of better poets than he who cannot scribble. To this end, he, the writer, must study his technical means—

An elucidation is the older term—but it refers more to an act than to a condition.

July 10.

Science is a sham to him who sees his city destroyed by gunfire. Philosophy is a cheat to him who has lost that which he loves and knows no better than to weep. Poetry at such moments is terrible, an overwhelming summation of life and the world—never perhaps to be set down, the type of a peculiarly humane knowledge.

Knowledge, as of certain women, a wife, a whore, a friend, enlarges by half the scope of the understanding; whereas of the broadest philosophy it can only be said that it has never penetrated beyond despair. It cannot be otherwise, the mistake having been to hunt in philosophy that outside which encloses it. Only a reflection could be real under such circumstances. The error occurs at the beginning —in not having defined first that for which the search has been made—not having placed it within a limit without which the search cannot begin since one of the terms is lacking—thus all the logic is nil. Let it be x?

Random Notes: Hello Madge.—I'm not Madge.—That's right. The reason I thought it was your sister is that your sister's better looking.

Nothing more savage than a young cat under a flowering catalpa tree.

Crows, herons and sea-gulls on the mudflats.

and the paths in the rushes the crabbers made by the stream's edge.

This that I am saying does not "solve" the difficulty. It does not solve anything. It discloses knowledge as humane—and of the character of men.

Mother of Moses there's a breeze, but it's all "hot air."

The Embodiment of Knowledge Etc.

IT IS TAKEN for granted in this thesis that the acquirement and possession of knowledge has an inhuman phase. It is called Science or Philosophy. Obviously knowledge itself is not involved since knowledge is the sine qua non of human achievement and success and must be always—science is to say "it has rained but it has not cleared off"—the acme of all that is human. It is in short a fetish—a fixed misconception or obfuscation—obscuring our view, which is our game, to be destroyed for the clarity which must ensue.

It is a rigorous adjustment which must be made before the acquirement of facts and a study of their relationships, a state of knowledge which when acquired must be as rigorously maintained throughout the series of steps succeeding which is scholarship. It is what is lacking in a college: the placing of the whole of knowledge which should be fixed in the first year—as it was placed by referring it to God in the earlier teaching, when in all our colleges the theological precept—or was most often the Dean—and as it is still in the Jesuitical schools.

The limits of the task must be set down in order to liberate the mind and not to enslave it—or else the search is at once unphilosophical and unscientific. The basis of all bad reasoning is in the beginning. All knowledge must be conceived as within the scope of human understanding; that is, *any* human understanding, therefore it is less than all or any, and its acquirement is a series within the scope of the mind. Older ages when spoken of as "good" no doubt referred to this—that men were the masters of their minds—that the fool, the idiot could be conceived as a creature.

It is to liberate the mind and so the human being from the tyranny of a blanketing misconception that is accomplished by this, the placing, direction, logic of a student—and to save the scholar from an inhuman poverty of wit.

It has rained a lot since the scientific revolution (and there has been a lot of philosophic thunder) but without clearing the atmosphere. We're far worse off than men seemed to be in the histories for we're discouraged whereas they were simply miserable.

This is the trap.—Either what we seek is within the bounds of the understanding or beyond it. If outside it does not exist for us, much less for our imagination; if inside it is bounded by that and must be so defined before it can be conceived.—This precedes all further progress. To conceive clearly the materials of our thought. Not that there is not that beyond our understanding but that until we have stated in comprehensible terms what it is that we would investigate and what we would discover within that whole, etc. The way out is for the mind to conceive itself as standing beyond its processes, so that if the process continue—

America or The Embodiment of Knowledge

So FAR, all serious discussions of knowledge have been from the viewpoint or view of scholarship. And at once I am in difficulty. For how can I know this to be so? I have neither the time, money, nor the ability—perhaps—to spend in an exhaustive search to make such a statement authoritative. I might be Shakespeare for all the help I could give.

Thus there is nothing to do, it seems, but accept the unproven statements as of equal weight with those of a life spent in research—or to acknowledge that there can never be a worthwhile discussion of knowledge save from the scholar's eminence—where he is so far above the vulgus that by his very scholarship he himself has become a curious species.

There is an analogy—A man who has committed a felony is before the court who must judge him. He is faced by another man of a different kind. It is of no interest to the court that the skillful lawyer striving in every way to break down the defense of the felon may himself be a blackguard, a wife beater, a lackey to some master, completely sold, a notorious liar and even a murderer—whereas the felon may have done no more than harangue a gathering of strikers. Everything in the wide realm of life is excluded from that court in order that, for a purpose, a certain deed may be discussed and ajudged. This must be so. But in the process a view of life, the embodied or actual view, is lost. The courts become an impertinence save for a purely chance discretion of the judge.

But our difficulty remains. How may one proceed and with weight in his words discuss something of which he

43

knows nothing? We can do so only by confining ourselves to what we know. For no life has seemed long enough for all knowledge. The scholar is but the final piece in a train going beyond sight into tradition. So he must always feel himself incomplete.

If, however, any man, a scholar, is incomplete in his generation he is less than some less-learned person who very actually finds himself, ignorantly no doubt, self-sufficient.

Obviously that is ridiculous. We can't do without proof. We can't do without knowledge. What then? We have to acknowledge first besides degrees and conditions of scholarship, that there is a division between those who know (some certain thing) and those who do not know it. We have to acknowledge then, that the scholar, not being ignorant, has not the knowledge which the ignorant man possesses. All that the wise man knows is colored by his wisdom. And all that the ignorant man knows is colored by his ignorance. But both are parts of a whole.

We must advance to a proof—which cannot be new—but one which scholarship has perhaps slighted. It is to say that in every man there is certain knowledge which by his life he proves, wise or a fool. He has in his own way proven it. An example of it being that the ignorant man finds the scholar's knowledge often disembodied. As the scholar finds himself, by his own knowledge, inhumanely cut off from his kind. Which he may despise or seek to serve, as he pleases. But it is knowledge which we are seeking to define.

The proofs I am approaching are those of a wider knowledge than any one of the divisions of humanity, learned or unlearned, has power to envision—it has to do with time—and the test of time, with color, diverse forms, contact of the senses—with style, invention—the creations of genius and of animals and flowers. Knowledge must be proven to us, not we to it. It must be universal to humanity, in some form permeable to everyone at once—in some form—or it is not true, and cannot be proven. In fact, that the proofs of scholarship are not proofs at all but trials in vacuo—at times, at least and best "type reactions."

It is that scholarship, unless it not recognize itself as being a special division of a logic which includes itself as one of its own parts, cannot hold any of its conclusions as valid—and when valid, only so when proven—upon humanity.

But to go on. It must be shown that men in general have in them the same sort of knowledge with respect to elevated understanding, that scholarship has to it. There must be this basis on which the two shall meet or no combining of them is possible and we have simply to acknowledge that humanity is split and of two kinds. It is not, of course. It should be possible for a professor of —— to discuss knowledge from a farmer, and to learn something to apply to his own sphere. It is.

And these, in still another field, are the cares, the distresses, the illuminations of art. For here is knowledge. And knowledge proven. Of universal appeal—or as near it as achieved—It is all sewed up together.

That if I am without proofs—they are without proofs also —which must be obvious to them since they know that until they know the whole no part can be likened to it.

But that there is a common basis of knowledge in which we can agree, and that if they want my proofs to them, they must first prove themselves to me, not by their proofs but by mine. Together, meanwhile, on equal grounds we have art.

Chapter One

My depressed and discouraged friends look at me with curious eyes. It is, I say to myself, the century. Most have cash. He who has once been happy is for aye out of destruction's reach. Why am I as I am? Understanding may be lack of wit. Of what use is my understanding and what is it that I have come to in the face of the world? This very note I happen to be writing at a cross street where once, in a field, I was seized by the throat, knocked down and kicked by an angry farmer, dead now, for running in and trampling his wheat. What is it all about? If I say to my friends: Poetry! they smile and look down. If I say America! they believe me insincere or provincial. Counsellors are remote. The college, looked back on, seems a delusion, the teachers paid tricksters. Church, the monotonous cruelty of women. The wisdom of the world is inaccessible—if it exist in an English translation. There is little but the plays of Shakespeare; almost nothing else. A slight knowledge of French, the sound of Spanish, etc.

Conversation has come to be impossible save among specialists in a certain pen, between the lists no language reaches. This is childish. Is there no conversation or communication between farmers and engineers? Strange to say I have found a very general language.

A very simple, easily worded abstract design: a clarity as gracefully put as I am capable of putting it with respect to the meaning. Not too short but not too long. A steady development of what I understand (Not stupid because I am not of the philosophers' guild) as well as I am able to think, and pretend no more. Then another design and so on to others to embody America and myself in it.

July 11.

It is an amazing thing that men believe their decisions somehow affect the course of the world. Certainly their lives are affected, who would be so rash as to believe that his life is important? And yet we believe it of the lives of others?

The answer seems to be that our decisions are important only relatively to each other within a sphere beyond which we forget it is always indefinitely possible to set up a new series and, of equal importance, where all the old remain intact and still operative—remain valid—perfectly valid since they have existed and were once so—quite as we are at times cats, hieratic priests—faintly or strongly, as it may happen. But the strangest proof is that we are capable [of] and even unable to avoid being obsessed by our high deductions exactly in the manner of the most primitive savage by a piece of black wood.

What in the world makes a man think that because he models his system after nature that he models it after sense— or that it is of more sense than another; or that the mind of man having gone through one phase cannot go through untold—or if not, that some other kind may not go differently. All of which signifies merely that there is man and within him an infinite series of variables—all of which means merely that one must stand somewhere outside of these things—in the manner of French painting—and that the academy is only one piece of furniture more.

July 10.

It should be possible to give a student, or one interested, an accurate, simple and concrete view of all knowledge in a few words, extremely plain (as the greatest abstractions are), of the world and of its parts and the various divisions of knowledge which he may undertake. Not a summary. This is a clarity. And it must stand in all accuracy for constant return and adjustment for all searchers. And if in research it be found to be inaccurate then it must be clipped and amended—and these later changes penetrate at once to the commencing student. The whole must be kept constantly in mind. An example in one category is the chemical table of Mendeleev—the basis of chemical deductions. All research must be within that sphere.

But no student nowadays is given to understand the meaning of knowledge (or of college)—a necessary view of the field—but is lost—brutalized by facts, brutalized by a sleet of information—deafened to a general language—dwarfed in understanding—made into a cock-eyed grotesque of a man to perform a given task:

Chapter Two

My own life-search for knowledge—avoid the sham. Would not every man, every boy, become a scholar—provided he did not see that it is an exclusion!

The Press.
The Intensely Human Bible—a defense and net for fools.
Scholars are sad—(Faust).
Shakespeare.
The Daredevil.

July 9.

The mind cannot have to do with that which lies beyond its sphere, therefore it behooves us to bring that which we wish to understand within the sphere of comprehension before we attempt to undo it. And thus before the mind goes always—and by necessity—the imagination.

This simplest precept is hardest to grasp and the source of greatest error (in Science and Philosophy) since it is at the fountain. The greatest difficulty is to state the difficulty, to state the problem in terms which can be investigated. Often, if we knew it, there is none other. But all through the modern depression of understanding, with its attendant schisms between men and men, runs this primal fault—and the value of the poet. It is to state—in the simplest possible, that is the most profound, terms, making us all brothers in the naturalness of our defects.

Chapter 4 6 9 Etc.

July 10.

The decay and disappearance—through lack of logical support—of the well-proven educational procedure of apprenticeship is due to a rational failure to realize at the start. The deceptive ideal of democracy with its attendant loss of human dignity is of the same root. Yet Rembrandt, Bach, Stradivarius must be classed on an equal plane with Galileo, Gregory—if understanding is to survive.

The worth was in clarity—when of a quality, then equal in all spheres.

The object of effort was better defined as that. But the scientific-philosophic mistake was in placing a mythical end to research at some remote future—toward which striving was inaugurated—comparable to a very identical "heaven" of mystical understanding, or the heaven of the stars presuming the unknown to be a fact. An error of understanding at the start.

In the apprentice system knowledge was a means, not an end—and it was consequently humane, logically based on a clarity as the culmination of understanding.

But our schools are based on the principle of a confused mass striving for the unseen summit of a topless cone—and that alone real. As a corollary, all save it is unreal. But as a fact only that which does not exist is unreal—that is, the unstated, unstatable—since nonexistent—end of our democratic ideal. So anxious are we to know something of everything, we have forgotten that all that can be known is the same in every category carried—clearly—to its end. That all we do by present teaching is to perpetuate confusion and despair, the highest product of our "education" being a Matthew Arnold, a Bertrand Russell or else, we must begin at once, on the completion of education, to forget it—if we have survived it at all—throw it off. But a pride in a craft is logically sound.

There is a subtle loss of dignity in saying a man is a poet instead of a scientist (this is a novel characteristic of the day due to the common misconception of learning and of poetry) as if—whereas it should be reversed: the poet knows what he knows but a scientist does not know what he knows.

(series) the scientific jargon has wasted the whole field— a work "enlarges the domain of beauty." To what end? "Pushes it further into the dark." As if enlargement—as if by being most large it would be more worthy. This idea of "size" is new. It does not produce Greek sculpture or architecture. Perhaps it is the aura of improbability which has made the scientists continue so profitably and links them with the alchemists so directly. Whereas before the experiment, they must know—to be scientific—the maximum limits of their intentions; and the alchemists who did not succeed because they neglected to state in clear terms what they postulated—the fact that lead *could* be changed to gold (dragged over from metaphysics whole piece) in the beginning of their experiments. Science, the legitimate child! making the same error. But if

July 13.

"They've got it down to a science, where there's nothing to it any more."

People cannot get used to the Jews: it is the persistence of a type out of phase. The Negro is another. In each case it is a phase which happens to coincide but roughly, by accident with the present—somewhat out of line.

The amazing shallowness of the classicist (and the acumen of such a man as Juan Gris when he said that the way to resemble the classics is to have performed work like them in nothing) is his failure to recognize that the Egyptian, the Greek or whatever of the past it may be is in its excellence the culmination of a phase, that the work is made up of parts elaborated by the phase itself—is the phase continuing in spore. But that to copy it, to make it of parts of a later phase is not only impossible but ludicrous. It is evidence of no penetration at all, it is shallow. They copy instead of to penetrate and find (if possible) a similar thing. In teaching "the classic" the student must be taught along with what he is learning that the classic *to him* is no more than a means— definitely to be thrown out when and if he is able to do so in favor of that part in the modern phase which parallels it. This should be kept in the forefront of teaching that he must throw out what he is being taught.

I wish it would stop raining. My brother's kids say they stopped the rain once.

How?

They just went out in their rain coats on the front lawn and said, Rain, rain, go away, come again some other day! and kept on saying it till it stopped.

Really!? Oh, I guess it was just going to stop anyway.

July 15.

I insist on the terminology: we are through with the comprehensive pretense of philosophy forever. It is just *one* of the branches of understanding, not an inclusion of understanding of them all. The position of the mind is *outside* all categories. There are these profound, interminable subdivisions, growing into a patent complexity. And there is clarity of understanding concerning them. Clarity. In the novel this clarity is shown in reduced circumstances among insignificant *hoi polloi* who by it are raised to a point of supreme interest and importance—above all the complex subdivisions—which they—though poor stuff—transcend.

Man must give himself without complete knowledge in the world—or he will not give himself at all. That is to say he will know—in his body—nothing at all.

August 4, 1928.

Admiration of scholars: etc. Upon what is our admiration for them and our disappointment, our perennial disappointment based? From their viewpoint, naturally, ignorance; from ours—our admiration is that they have achieved a clarity with respect to life as a whole—especially in the cases of philosophers and religious leaders; whereas they prove to be little men confused, narcotized by their information.

Proof is often an odd time-destroyer. Men have always tried to bridge the gap between assumption and proof by the presentation of the theory, the theorem; an assumption in interim taken to be true so that we may get to work whereas, as in the various axioms on which all mathematics is based, there may never be any proof at all. Yet we must make the choice between no mathematics at all or the assumption that it is true until it is proven false. But often a whole series of presumably true assumptions on which a generation of work has been based is proven false: such as the obvious one that the universe was geocentric or the other, neither proved nor disproved, that there is a humanistic if not a man-shaped god above. What of it? All manner of knowledge and effort has been based on these two assumptions, none could wait for proof. Is it proved, for instance, that medicine, as a science, will not finally accelerate the destruction of the race by pouring vitiated blood into the human veins whereas it seems quite plain that the driving purpose of disease is to rid the race of worthless lumber? These things are not proven yet men believe they can proceed by proof alone and only so fast as proof supports reason. It is inhuman to do so.

With science our admiration may be somewhat differently based in a practical age, much as we would admire a man who could lift a larger barrel than can we.

Goldfish Varieties etc. Wm. T. Inness. Inness & Sons, Publishers, Phila.

I'm going to take a vacation.
I suppose it'll be a little one. Youse doctors don't get much time, it's like us mothers. I have a little store but I can't do a thing.

Why do I live in the town in which I was born? I who am a gypsy by inheritance and personal preference. Because one clarity is like another. To know all towns of greater or less degree to which I may go. If I go out and see I want to know all I see—as far as I please, I want to know what I want to know, need to know for my personal satisfaction.—

It is characteristic of children that they want to know everything at once. So it should be told them. Great knowledge tends toward simplification of understanding, so to be succinct in what we have to tell children would be the genius of a teacher. Everything should always be taught at once: the entire field of knowledge every year widening. The curiosity should be satisfied and the interest watched with selective attention.

And suppose all my little, apish, amateurish logic is wrong. What of it?

I won't get a divorce. I'm not going to spoil my kids' names just for his lousy pleasure.

Chapter One

THERE WAS ONCE a Harvard professor, so I have heard, who could tell to within twenty miles, by their accent alone, the locality whence his students had come. The elder Morgan is said to have had the power, by one look of the eye, to fix the precise cash value of any man or woman he encountered. Johns Hopkins the same, and [a] clerk in many a small store the same. There are wine tasters who, blindfold, detect the place and year of origin of any wine placed before them with a nearly perfect score. Indians in spearing a fish allow for refraction by the water and aim not at the false image but at the spot where the fish will be. Père Rasles, I think it was, speaks of being with an Indian on the hunt. Two deer trails crossed. To determine which was the fresh one the savage scooped up the soil from a hoof print. He smelled it intently. Doing the same with the other he unerringly picked the right track and the deer they were pursuing was shortly overtaken. The story of Ehrlich is that while he was away his laboratory assistant—perhaps to show his knowledge—rearranged the bottles of reagents in systematic order according to their chemical affinities. When the old man returned for work he was powerless until all had been restored to its former formal disorder. These are my texts. But if one should turn to women seeking a mate, the category could be elaborated and variegated into a veritable allegory of existence, no doubt.

Let it be as it may with a man's life, if his writings be good it is a depository of strength for the freedom of his spirit against the economists who would freeze him into their successful schemes. Dying—or retiring into a shell-hole to exist—miserably as a soldier, shelled at and shot at by machine guns of the successes—a man may live dangerously —but well in spite of everything and his writings may be the thing that will win—or be a mausoleum.

And there is a battle to preserve such writing. It may fall under the careful attack, fail to be published, fail to survive because of lack of reviews, appreciation, and if so it is a loss to the spirit.

Such writing is McAlmon's. It will not be measured by the scales of politeness. A determined and persistent campaign must be made to preserve them.

All sciences and philosophies, all the various categories of intellectual investigation and in metaphysics. Art alone remains always concrete, objective.

Children

THE AMAZINGLY interesting and continuously satisfying thing about children is that they are not small adults but a race by themselves. It took the Greeks a long time to recognize the correct proportions between a child's head and his total body length; at first they used the adult ratio in making a child. Primitive people partly recognize this in the elf and gnome myths—just kids. Really they are not small at all but full size. Only the most superficial conception compares them with adults: a whole world in itself.

Daring

WHEN PENN had defeated Harvard in 1905 after several lean years Dr. White who was a great football enthusiast was congratulating Bob Torrey as captain of the team on his success. Dr. White was professor of Surgery at Penn, Bob was a medical student—I'd give everything I own to be in your position right now, said Dr. White. Torrey thought a moment. No, he said finally, I wouldn't trade with you, because now I am what I am and later I may be what you are.

Youth by daring and athletic exertion achieves clarity. It is notable that of that famous team at Penn, Torrey gave first honors to Malcolm Stevenson whose sharp rasping voice calling the signals during the silences of the game preceding certain scrimmages soothed the attentive ear of every student in the stands as it brought fear to the enemy and confidence to our own linesmen and backs. This is the same man who was driven from the university in his second year for failure in scholarship and general insubordination. The whole campus was continually distressed and exalted by his fame and lost deeds.

Dr. Casamajor—Youths praise, despise learning, interpret, clear it.

[The Burden of Proof]

(end of #1) Such a situation presents great difficulties to the logic of an attack such as I assume, for without valid logic or as close to it as we can get nothing is serious, we would have to assume that the scholar is the only one who can ever write of these things with authority, and the book ends where it begins.

It is precisely upon these difficulties that I build my understanding and offer my appeal. It is to hold the scholar strictly to his rules that frees me. For just as he requires of me certain formal requisites before I can enter his field, so do I now require the same of him before he can enter mine or he stops where he begins and he remains isolated and unable to proceed. I demand, as pure logic, that he must first know all concerning man or he cannot prove his effects. In having knowledge he has an apple. What of it? Just as knowledge perfectly illogically establishes itself regularly against every student, every man in turn who approaches it —and if no man approaches it it ceases to exist—asking him to prove this that or the other. So, far more logically, I assume the man as fixed to which knowledge must approach him by proofs of his terms or be rejected as wholly illogical and beside the point.

Thus by reversing the current, putting the burden of proof upon the dynamic bodies of facts rather than the inhuman one of brutalizing the man by measuring him up to an accumulation of traditional ideas, there is opened a way to proceed which, if not reaching out like so many chiseled steps, is yet quite as logical as the usual process of scholars, but to reverse them, to turn them back whence they originally came to the man himself. Thus we can build upon the very obstacles which seem to block the way.

Let scholarship learn *me*, proving itself to me step by step, holding to its very rigid precepts of demonstration and proof as strictly as I will see that it shall. Thus on that ground, with authority, I proceed, to discuss it as I need, for here *I* am set down and what my world is, of which Science is a small part. It cannot swing me and never could, an age-old fetish, not tyrannical need.

But all proof can easily be shown to be a vain thing. The chief object of all thought being to remove obstacles. Proof is very near to a trick—that [a man] may not be blocked— but go on with what he intends in coming to grips with his world. The laborious processes of scholarship are a bar when they make life futile with a crushing burden of proofs. The trick is to get such burdens out of the way, placing them in the place, out of the main current. No one can be deceived that they are not necessary to scholars—in their category they are supreme. It is only when they have gotten out of hand and lie in the roads and we mill around them like ants or as men have been doing about science and its machines and discoveries, that something must supercede them for the moment, call it life, humanity with a simpler logic—clearing the way.

(paragraph 3)

This is plainly not scholarship, neither is it a man. It is writing about knowledge which must seize a sanction before it can seriously proceed, valid in the eyes of scholarship itself.

I am sick and tired of piecemeal criticisms of life—of proofs that are no proofs at all. How in the world can knowledge set up its "scientific," "philosophic" measurements as sacrosanct rigidly, tyrannically above me when everything it does denies them *as a whole*. I assert that the whole is greater than all its parts and that since no one knows anything about it all proofs are invalid—as prohibitions—except relatively to its own set of conditions and *ad interim* while one must proceed, as always, with the business of existence by measures always greatly in question, but unless whole, always, of sufficient dignity always to warrant every notice, man in the seat of his own power—then nothing exists in the parts of his exercises which can be anything but insignificant and unworthy of him. It is a fetish, an aspect of stupidity and powerlessness when any part, even the part of knowledge itself, can supersede man with its monkeylike "proofs" so that he lies on his back and fears to cross its chalk lines. But nothing can be forced. We must stick to the proven rules, as far as they are proven, and for themselves, but beyond them exists something else.

(paragraph #4)   This is not a book of proofs—least of all no book of scholarly proofs; it is a presentation, an exposition of the title "The Embodiment of Knowledge" from the point of view of man which is supposed, as such, to be incapable of proofs or at least to proceed without them—everywhere, which is quite true.

This is no more an attempt to solve anything—least of all humanity or knowledge as a thesis in itself. It is—to restate more simply if possible what I have said above—an elucidation of the relationship between humanity and the body of knowledge as it exists in the world and to relieve both of what seems to me a burden of misunderstanding as it exists between them—to the bewilderment of both and the mischief of the former in especial.

So much for an appeal for tolerance before the court—deference requires this much for one thing depends on the other and to drive them apart—even in the confines of a discussion—would be the opposite of the purpose.

[The Embodiment of Knowledge]

1.

KNOWLEDGE is something separate from man as a creature. It is something of varying proportions possessed here and there brokenly. One may exist without great sections of it, though not well. In the aggregate the tribe of men are supposed to possess all of it at any moment though not operative—necessarily.

Together we have it, separately we may suffer severely for the lack of it. We carry it about and present it one to the other if we are so inclined or forced so to do by circumstances. It is something separate from man, without which he still exists, unless all men and all knowledge be taken together.

But to realize knowledge as a thing apart from any one man we have only to remember that he may be without it, get it—sometimes at great pains, give it and lose it. Having held it momentarily, as a discovery, to feel it slip off and then to see it disappear in the possession of someone else may not be lightly taken. It may be fatal.

Machinery as an effect of complicated knowledge has many aspects to the individual—some of which show it to be out of hand. That is, there are aspects to machinery quite apart from the technical ones involved in its mechanical conception, practicalization and operation. It is mystery just as patent as the virgin birth until it be solved and man replaced in knowledge above it. As soon as we make it we must at once plan to escape—and escape. By this we understand the escape of man from domination by his own engines. Thus continually he asserts himself above what he knows and which has tended to fix him as part of itself. To stop before any machine is to make of it a fetish attended by its metaphysical priest the engineer. It is not necessarily to be an engineer to conceive the place of a machine, nor is it easy to escape them: On the contrary the knowledge of an engineer, being so in particular, is likely to absorb him into itself until he becomes a scientist—limited, segregated —unable to escape.

But knowledge itself is just such a machine.

The embodiment of knowledge can have no meaning but the escape of man from its domination as a fetish of knowledge itself by realizing its function and its place as subordinate to himself—oddly metaphysical as it may sound.

It is hardly necessary for me on the other hand to state, in this context what man is—provided he can be shown to exist above his own schemes.

Everything else but man I will however propound is metaphysical: science, philosophy, anything you will—save perhaps art either as cheese or music or love.

Knowledge is essential, delightful, human—as that you should never wash a pie plate or a rolling pin; science, as the codified sum of knowledge is stupid and inhuman— unless we achieve toward it the same relationship that we find most essential, delightful, human, in any of its parts. Unless we stand beyond it and not it beyond us to order us, it is no more than an evidence of our ignorance, in all its perfection, another machine whose scope apart from the mere practical one of wheels going around and moulding tin or dough—we have not surmounted. It is plain ignorance, the modern deception, in fact the most modern, as philosophy is the oldest but of the same sort.

These are things to use. Men have forgotten that merely because they have discovered no end to which to use them. No end, that is, but to fill his needs. Failing that, he has quite plainly feared them, worshipped them in the persons of others and finally succumbed to the taboo—quite the same as before a hollow log of ebony or other delightful piece of timber which art alone knows how to estimate— much to the amazement of all the world but artists.

What kind of a mind—since after all a mind is not knowledge or scholarship—is most likely to make useful discoveries in these matters? Precisely not the scientific or philosophic one which is involved in its exercises just as a hieratic priest is involved in his ritual or a mediaeval preacher in his dogma, but the mind which will be humane in its perceptions and skilled in transverse, not perpendicular ways. The earth is round.

The effect of education is surely to keep us, as Americans, from each other; the history we are taught is particularly blank—or rather the history we are not taught is terrifying when one looks back at the years that have been spent solely to keep us ignorant. But the chief effect of it all is to have allowed time to pass during our most impressionable years without coming into contact, actually, with what has happened and is happening around us.

1.

"only impertinence could lead him to dispute or discuss the principles of any science."

2.

"Adams knew nothing of any of them, but—all reacted on his mind."

Had I received the policy you say you sent me July 11—along with a letter—I should have returned it at once; since I have never received either there is nothing for me to do but to tell you how things stand and trust to you to do what you find necessary to straighten matters out.

"In wandering through the forests of ignorance."

The theory of college seems to be to keep a young man working so hard that he can find out nothing but what he is being taught. While his own object must be, if he have a mind at all, to find out what relation, if any, college has to his life by knowing and finding out as much as possible outside of his studies.

AUGUST 22.
(first pages—addenda)

But poetry—the writing—is more than just another in the series (of poetry as the apex of knowledge in any category). It is the type but it is also the apex and purity of the type in itself, more so than music. Furthermore it has an immediate coloration; it is the active denial of what science and philosophy, religion or whatever else it may be—pretend. And it is the affirmation of the basis, of what knowledge is, neglected by them—the purest, most accurate form of what it is to know. It caps music which fails where it seems just at the point of success, and most expressive, by its inarticulateness, requiring the words of songs; as the poetry gains just that expressiveness which music serves at the same time, but is never heightened more articulate.

Poetry is the one purely articulate form, more so than action which involves the mind so scantily, or to know. Beside it the great climaxes of science seem like the clumsiest camel troopings.

—one may, take the chance, that he is right (just as mathematics is founded on unproved axioms) and proceed with his arguments. If he is wrong his work may have the virtue, at least, of proving him so. And if he is right, without proof, it will become the duty of those whose duty it is to prove him so. At best he may prove interesting for his style and observations, at worst, if he retain a proper modesty, he has wasted his time.

—seduced by their discovery of an order in nature which seems to be a direction—even an incitement to rush upon the conclusion that there is a unity, which appears as an end—

[Bacon and Shakespeare]

IT IS NOT probable, however that [Bacon] had as simple an idea to guide him as I have intimated. It is correct to think that he along with others started the fiction of science to add to its actuality of simple act of discovery and deduction. They were seduced, etc. It is highly probable that science was tinctured by the metaphysics and religious beliefs of the time (as Darwin was also at a later date) into believing that it had found a system which it had only to follow in order to come out into a blinding and comprehensive fullness which would be the sum of all the ages had acquired, carefully built into a noble "temple," the "temple of Science"—or whatever it may be.

This is the fiction which has infested the minds of all great men, the alluring bait which has drawn them on.— And that is its truth. It could be shown that all necessary work begins in fiction, the glow of the mind which carries it forward. Bacon and his confrères of the period had a great work to do. Science had to be built up. The lure of a solution of life carried them forward giving them the belief that to know everything was the end of knowledge, the same falsity that debauches the mind of a college boy to this day. It had a perfect justice as an incentive to work and has worked so wonderfully.

But truths of that sort (or any sort—as Ibsen pointed out) endure little over twenty years. This one is now so old, so worn, so violently wrong that its viciousness has become surely the most distorting, obsessive ghost of the world. It is the most violent lie in existence to the extent that it has been the most powerful force inciting men to labor for hundreds of years. Now it must be killed. It must be killed by showing it false. This is why Science—for that is what "science" has come to mean, the fiction itself, and Philosophy—for it is the same there—must be branded as lie.

If any truth of the day could be more far-reaching than this or more promising of good—at once—

In this light the—

At the same period existed another who professed knowledge of another sort, the unevangelical Shakespeare. And the fact that he also possessed knowledge along with Bacon; the fact that he possessed knowledge almost anonymously, since no one bothered to preserve his record, has created all kinds of silliness and confusion in the minds of later scholars.

Bacon was avowedly brilliant and he stood besides at the head of a movement destined to come down through the centuries as one of the most fruitful in the history of the world. He was distinguished clearly in his day. He was at the head of the new. He was the radical. But the obscure Shakespeare who also possessed knowledge possessed it without the dream. He knew purely. Thus his work is incapable of systematization, in the best modern, that is the oldest, sense. His knowledge is incapable of false arrangements copied after subtle inductions of nature. He was bent on an entirely different, more primitive, more modern track than Bacon. It would be impossible to find two minds more widely separated. In nothing did they resemble each other, as their styles, their written styles, clearly show.

For Shakespeare there served the earliest model for pure knowledge, poetry, in the active form of the drama. The plays of Shakespeare are a reserve at the present moment of greater force—bulk than ever, in that they stand at the entrance to the Baconian era to which we return for a summary.

Poetry is the one form that Shakespeare's knowledge could assume that his plays might be a document—so little thought of that they almost disappeared—might present a case sensitively appreciated by everyone, even when they did not know why, for knowledge. It is as knowledge that they have most value, as the handy farmer would build a barn, not without art, to keep the animals in.

[Philosophy, Science and Poetry]

Since I have not the reading or even the memory of what I have read to be exhaustive I must say that if an error is detected in one location it is likely and very nearly certain that the same error will be found under similar circumstances elsewhere and in other things. Also that isolated statements unrelated by thought, detected here and there— if what I find be true—will be related in a new way and though the tapestry, so to speak, may not be completed, due to my lack of means, yet the design may be indicated.

Such a statement is the one from a Sunday newspaper, that philosophy is simply thought that has been thought out. Splendid but quite untrue unless it be understood after the principle which I am forwarding, which has not been the case to date. Philosophy in every case has been thought thought out in relation to a scheme which purports to elucidate knowledge and [to] detail the object of life as a complex whole making part of a great unity. This is far from "thought thought out." It is thought followed in order to find an end, a logical culmination, definite and material in the terms of the equation. But it has ended as chemistry in the proposition that motion is matter and matter motion, the tailing off into infinities after the manner of mathematics—or else it has taken on the humanistic aspect of use to an end. As either of these things it is dead as philosophy, as knowledge.

But there is a new alignment into which the chance statement recovered above will fit. It is that knowledge is not at the end of the deduction but in each phase of it and everywhere. Thus philosophy becomes exactly thought that has been thought out but in being acknowledged so, the exact term, philosophy, as usually understood, disappears. And we see that thought that has been thought out becomes simply knowledge.

That is that the term "philosophy" as an art practiced by philosophers was based, like science, on a false assumption, a hieratical accumulation peculiar to their guild and inaccessible to the rest of men, such as myself. Therefore that no one was permitted, logically so long as the definition holds, to comment upon it save he have been first to transport a term from another field and a futile one, one of those that inhabit the "sacred wood."

But if, as I seek to show, the achievements of philosophy are not what philosophers believe but of the same sort as the "thoughts thought out" of any man or woman, all such thoughts are linked in a new series running transverse to the old. In each process is all the knowledge there is. Thus any man may with full knowledge attack any philosophic situation, as to its basis, provided in his own field he be one who has experienced knowledge. He is merely lower in the series but he is in the same series which "philosophers" pursue and not to be excluded. Nor need a humanitarian view—which is something else—be taken,—and has nothing to do with philosophy at all—unless a new definition be accepted.

With the result at the end of a laborious process, whereas it is in each step. And though it may be at the end also, this will not be of a different kind, and proof does not exist.

Philosophy, history, are well enough but if you want to know anything actual about man, about a man, a woman, how they will act under all conditions—in love, after his head has been cut off, you go to poetry—to Dante, to Donne. This is knowledge, this is the knowledge that the others mirror. All other presentation uses writing to speak about something else, as in the writing of philosophy wherein the philosophers themselves are frequently mistaken since they are not primarily writers. But poetry is all of a piece, knowledge presented in the form of pure writing which is made of the writing itself.

There is a unity, of course, and the final term of all investigation; it is the individual himself. Anyone must have as his fundamental determination a complete association of all the activities of his life and their implications. It is the various implications which constitute the sciences, arts, philosophies and so forth. But the unity they seek is behind them not before. Before them exists only an infinite fracture, an ever smaller division until—as in chemistry the constitution of an electron, or in astronomy ever farther and larger objects (to reverse the process) puts objective investigations beyond the question. By further investigation, that is to say, unity is not by any means achieved, but multiformity.

But if a man take one of the implications of his own unity as a track for his effort all the others are implied because of a relation back to the source and each act in that course, implying all others, and thus the man himself has what he has always desired, unity accomplished. For what it is worth, this is all the unity attainable.

Thus a man wishes to know all there is in his life as a result of his own unity, the immediate result of which is to push him further and further in his mastery of some craft, some art, some investigation which, as he grows older, more experienced, evolves as it is said, becomes more comprehensive and at the same time as far as he himself is concerned becomes simpler and simpler. Thus it is more complex to the beholder of an artist painting a picture as he approaches mastery, but within himself, since it shows itself more and more as the type of all his desires, it approaches unity or as it is said, more expressive of what he is himself. When he might be conceived to have achieved perfect unity of effect he must be at the end of his activities—and hence the tragedy.

There has never been an adequate definition of poetry, a

defect which shows itself in nearly all criticism from that of the *Criterion* School of an Eliot to the usual Sunday Edition estimate of a new book of verse by some young man or woman. It is related to nothing, valued in several currencies, none of which seems to have a measurable value. There is no rule for the *Iliad*, the "Anatomie" of Donne and the work of H. D.

Many definitions have been attempted within the limits of what is called prosody in the grammars; metaphysical explanations have been given, particularly with reference to the Christian poets; attempts have been made to define poetry on the basis of its rhythmic and metaphorical character; color has been invoked, etc., etc. But these are all variations within the type and explain nothing. These are all really the effect of speed or of the intensities involved, especially with reference to the rhythm which affects words as it does sand or whatever else is subject to motion. It is to be explained by physics and not grammar.

The definition sought will have to be on larger grounds. Poetry must be defined not by its superficial features but by its character as an effect related to science and the other categories. As knowledge in a certain form. Poems must be —and this partakes of technique—considered as documents of men. Thus, without seeking a pungent example for the moment—new works must be based—or their criticism—on an increase of knowledge, and will be accepted or rejected solely upon that score. But it is their bodies as poems, as with men, that is their destiny, differing from all writing which has not writing itself as its substance.

The first effect of which is to certainly define the great poem from the ordinary one—difficult as it may be to recognize the difference in the original. The great or actual poem is the one which in its body is an increase in knowledge. Whereas poems have a lesser or formal value also as they repeat the advancing work.

The analogy between the poem and the scientific advance is here again of use.

Shakespeare is so to be judged. So too is the explanation why at the beginning of a movement, when a new form is set, the chief poems are created. It is not novelty, though of necessity the great must [be] the new, it is the increase of knowledge that is the deciding point.

Or, if not the increase of knowledge in an absolute sense, it may be the representation of knowledge from an illegible script.

In this presentation of a new theory of knowledge no attempt will be made to solve specific difficulties of thought since that is not the intention but to influence all thought. All that will be attempted will be to show how knowledge may be related to the individual in a new way.

Anyone acquainted with the grave and beautiful processes of science—even if no more so than to the extent of having read Ivan Pavlov's first one hundred pages on the "Conditioned Reflexes," and especially anyone who has known such men as Erdheim—must go slow.

Apology

It was richly rewarding when the other day, in a Vermont farmhouse, in excellent translation, I came upon Luigi da Porto's early sixteenth-century story of Juliet and Romeo. Shakespeare was ignorant of this original. My interest was not in that however, nor in the edition, which was a cheap one, nor in anything of the usual scholarly or antiquarian note. I felt that I had acquired rare knowledge, but knowledge of a certain stamp, general in bearing, which I had been seeking to bring to a stand upon some one thing for several weeks. I had been seeking to prove to myself a new character in the knowledge itself and now I had hit upon something which went definitely home. Shakespeare was set off in a strong northern light by the Italian's account. He became rude, English. His own version of the old story took on a special coloration, a certain contour that I had been unable to perceive hitherto and which I welcomed. It was less delicate, less tender, more sentimental, wordier. The Italian was swifter, subtler in emotion, less ornate, far more real. In fact the very breath of reality seemed to come from the Italian account. Both versions benefited. It seemed a new criticism.

But I do not wish particularly to speak of literature. It is the kind of experience which this involves that held me. In all it was as clear an experiment as one could wish to see in chemistry or mathematics. Knowledge itself seemed defined in a new and unmistakable manner. There was a roundness which granted several diameters which could be named science, philosophy, history, literature—all of which must be an aspect of this thing. I felt it and saw it definitely before me. I felt satisfied.

No doubt the satisfaction was in having objectivized the rather vague conviction which is the force which this thesis seeks [to,] must expose. All that follows will be no more than to elucidate what is there and in as many parts as seen. But unfortunately I cannot go on in this way—and do not wish to do so. The character of knowledge and the stupidities which corrode it, have long seemed to me the first point of attack before anyone can go on with anything worthy to be called knowing.

Nobody knows anything, in America at any rate [this] has always seemed the take-off for the first serious experience which must be undertaken, and the beginning of that is in the mistaken character of knowledge itself.

Certainly it would be nice to pick up pebbles all one's life or philosophic facts the same and—truly—some apology must be offered when I determine plainly not only not to do so but to go at once into theory. For pieces of knowledge such as that which I have demonstrated are of little more use than pebbles. And all knowledge is the same. To pretend more is in the briefest possible way the defect which I would destroy, with what benefits to knowledge itself as may become apparent as I am able to go on.

Apologize I will, notwithstanding, to those who are rich. Anyone, to the advancement of knowledge itself, as knowledge cleared of legend and incidentally—and perhaps only incidentally humanized.

But this requires walking indifferently in science, philosophy, literature—wherever one is led or happens to find it possible to go. For it is the very universal character of all knowledge that I pursue, that the character of any piece of knowledge is the same and that its superficial aspects only are called scientific, philosophic, literary, or whatever it may be. This does require an apology from anyone who has faced the world and knows even vaguely of its complexity and the character of skilled application.

Anyone who has read even the first one hundred and fifty pages of Ivan Pavlov's *Conditioned Reflexes*, etc., must look at me as an interloper on sacred fields. I know little or nothing of Philosophy. Yet if these hierarchies are not penetrable by the means I wish to employ—then I fail. That they are so by knowing, by knowing anything which of itself grants a certain insight into knowing special things and makes them applicable and to the point.

It is a theory in plain words, which I will advance with what application I may, rather than by seeking to accumulate instances for which I have not the time, the cash for leisure, the ability, perhaps, to go further and absolutely not the taste or conviction that it will do, any more than I have the taste for cash, which if I had it—? So as I may I say what I can. At most, it may be, it is an autobiography of one who has a small knowledge which is sought. At worst it is a waste of time—possibly diverting. Certainly it will be diverting to me or I should not undertake it.

Charming, loveable and especially able and devoted men, one can not speak [to] violently, especially uninformedly—in their fields—though one may, against the law—walk across them without getting a load of buckshot.

I begin with a few general and perhaps untenable statements. Philosophy is a sham, etc.

In the field of disarranged information at most, places where what I have to state may be found true or at least applicable. It is an apology—frankly, failing better. But at best a clarity must be shown to strike through it if it strike anywhere—a

Philosophy

> "Our age has lost much of its ear for poetry, as it has its eye for color and line, and its taste for war and worship, wine and woman."

QUITE THE OPPOSITE, we know everything. Or should. Or have known.

Without undue stress I take the second statement to be correct, the first incorrect. As indicative of what is meant.—

Multiplicity offers this difficulty to all solutions, philosophic among others (and the refuge of humanity—as of trees) (as of Saints) that in the case of any man—the knowledge of each precept of philosophy and so of philosophy must be re-enacted for him before it exist. Each proposition of philosophy is not proven until it has been proven in each case. The adductions of each man are knowledge balanced by knowledge in every other man, having actuality by *that* in other men and equal (tho' dissimilar) knowledge. Knowledge, I wish to point out, is the coin. Gains its value by a gift as between each man.—

Others may acquire the facts philosophers have deduced. But it must be pointed out that he who has acquired the knowledge at first has a distinction over his fellows which the acquirement of all subsequent knowledge (on top of it) does not dim. It is because knowledge and philosophy (the partial term) are distinct.

The old school proposal, that any graduate of a modern technical school knows more than Euclid, is tenable only on conventional grounds. It seems not unreasonable to be-

lieve according to my second statement that Euclid knew
infinitely more tho' his necessities for the acquisition were
less.

In the same vein a bird knows more of a tree than man
ever will. An Indian knew more of fire than the designer
of the Bessemer smelter. Or rather both cases knew the
same.

It is certain at least that Praxiteles knew—that the man
25,000 years ago when he scratched and painted the image
of a white rhinoceros, covered with tic birds, on the wall
of his rocky cave in Western Transvaal—knew—

Were I to wish to demonstrate equal knowledge it would
be by doing (in that category, that is—design) something
as opposite to my day as the white rhinoceros, *i.e.*, some-
thing entirely different.

That is in accord with the saying of Juan Gris, etc. And
for this reason I have always felt and add that art is infi-
nitely more able—and more worthy of a man than philoso-
phy or science—today.

Still Philosophy and Science accumulate their threads of
facts, their "solutions" and ignoring completely—multiplic-
ity (the most patent thing in the world), that to be knowl-
edge it must exist in each case—of necessity—as art does,
(points of this that drove some French genius mad)—there-
fore it has *not* the universal currency and permeability
which they believe.

It is knowledge that is the universal (donator) that gives
a thing value, universal transmutability. Not philosophy (I
stick to my term). It is knowledge, different in each class
(case), that alone solves multiplicity. It is knowledge that
is the basis of art—that knows how to change and acknowl-
edge the multiple-variability of its coin. Transcends time
instead of layers of superimposed and oppressive values,
gives an equal value, *i.e.*, we know, or have known every-
thing.

What then do the accumulations of Science and Philoso-
phy (which art ignores), all the stuff of the books amount

to? That it is valuable, useful, we know. This is unfortunate, since apart from that it is worth nothing. Did we not, we, by *our* ability (not its virtue) give it coinage for what we animally need, it would be seen to be a stone of stupidity. We know everything, all that halts us (such accumulations as these—books) are pseudo-knowledge (save as we give them our power—uniquely possessed in multiple—to live—knowledge).

Then why the stress of learning and schools?

To know.

Henry Adams speaking of the acceleration of life hits a phase—today. When the phase is finished (coal or whatever) an infinite number may supervene. Multiplicity and variability are the fruits of knowledge.

It is a too-small world that imagines its solution by abstract deductions. They have value but only after reservations of the severest kind.

What vista does philosophy bring to mind?

Is it not a field partly known which when finally we have accomplished the design we shall know all?

Nothing could be more false—stultifying. For what of fields beyond that—and other fields?

But it is false far and above even that base. Nothing more stultifying. It is responsible—more than death (to which it has given a false color) for the postponement of knowledge of life which is a major predicament of the mind today. It *will* be when—etc., etc.

The second statement gives a different vista. To know, to know death. There is a different aspect at once. The field of postponement is removed. To know is everywhere, teeming, at once, in anything. And it is all here in any life. Criminal perhaps, but present. Even the jazzy present has this virtue that, low as it is, it is a prediction of a new order of knowing. Men are not content to accept the postponements of science and philosophy which they with sure instinct reject. But they do not know how to interpret their find. But it is right, fine. Tho' for the moment it is low—uncertain—too much in controversy with the melting past.

The war—

> Science finds out ingenious ways to kill
> > Strong men and keep alive the weak and ill—
> That these a sickly progeny may breed,
> > Too poor to tax, too numerous to feed.

It is true. It is catastrophic. No man has been able to remove it or understand it or stop it. Medicine is sick with it. Its only possible excuse, is transition. In order to get a type the whole genus must go through—or down. The type will be of a certain head. The body will then be brought up to that—

The war stupid—philosophically correct as can be shown historically, biologically salutary—and inevitable—was wholly without dignity save that of men—

The logical conclusion, or *reductio ad absurdum*—as it may be—is that when philosophy (or science) has solved the complexities of the ultimate constitution of matter—we shall somehow know more than the man who drew the white rhinoceros on the West Transvaal wall.

It is unlikely.

["Humanization" vs. "Utilization" of Knowledge]

1.

MAY I point out at the start the difference between The Humanization of Knowledge and the Utilization of Knowledge—as two things with the first of which only will I have to do.

It is knowledge itself as a material with which I have to do. To acquire it is the sole object of science and philosophy. To study knowledge as a fact established and to criticize the studied attitude toward it. With a view to showing misconceptions which render it un-human—and to that very extent false—is the object of my work. By which it is implied that knowledge (apart from its utility) is completely human, except by its false conception—necessitated by transitory conditions (now over-ripe) so to define falseness, by time.

One need not humanize it. It is human, purely. But only the misconceptions foisted on that concept are false. Clear them away and knowledge is human, thus humanized, purely—and nothing else.

The vista which Philosophy and Science bring up is one of terror—but that has no founding, even in Philosophy of nothingness, remoteness, insignificance of man, despair—infinite postponement, inhumanity and the end.

But this has nothing to do with knowledge—which pretends nothing.

They say the science of medicine is humane. It is not so —but most inhuman in its conception.

Prose Essays
1914–1929

(1) BUT TO THIS HABIT, this congeniality for the sterilities of Science and Philosophy, if I attribute perversions of life, impasses, stupidity—no one will be inclined to go further, to say flatly that to the scientific age are due the defects we complain of—to science: an uproar is caused.

(2) But if on the other hand I seek to maintain that Science and Philosophy have spent their force in a vain attempt to prove their tenets and that the truth lies elsewhere, outside of their sphere, a neglected corrective—in the category of art: If I say Science and Philosophy "are lies" the thesis is considered preposterous. We are not used to the terms of such an approach to knowledge. The other is more congenial to us.

(3) To look where we would encounter a class of reasons —those of art—with which we would not be familiar—of a different sort from those of Science and Philosophy—none the less true. As the prediction of the war in the work of Hartley in Berlin and Picasso in Paris.

(4) They may. W. Lewis lays out at Ezra Pound that he is lacking in intellect, without originality and in love with the past, referring doubtless to Pound the admirer of W. Lewis influenced by Picasso and Joyce. But we are convinced by this pander because, by God, what he says is scientifically and scientifically true. We buy his book. Whereas the truth, that is, Pound's body of verse, sensitively, superlatively making a head to the man, we ignore— apart from its truth or untruth—it is just a piece of irrelevancy—it is not a statement in the category of art which it seeks to engage, or wherein it seeks to engage its subject.

But we are *inclined* to treat it as sense rather than to investigate—by reading the verse, by entering another field, the actual field of the subject. Pound's verse.

(L) Science and philosophy have become in our day the anatomy and physiology of a body lacking the head.

The predominant influence upon our lives attributable to these two categories of understanding has grown notwithstanding, greater and greater, to the virtual exclusion of other categories—notably art—is demonstrable daily. The injury is however not realized, so bent are our best minds in absorbing pursuits—which preclude thought—save—to a philosophic or scientific end.

As a confusion of categories is the most flagrant error in discussions of art so it is the first defense of the philosophically or scientifically minded against the artist and art itself. A common one is a criticism of art based on the current Freudian classifications (which Proust by superlative art surely must have blasted, would one look clearheadedly at the remote and at the same time primary significance of his work: a subject treated in a superlative manner in a given category, not scientific, not philosophic but art. How much better treated than by Freud—just as pure knowledge, a brilliance in the newer realm of knowledge) of the artist's mentality—an obvious absurdity as far as artistic criticism is concerned—since the action *never enters* the field it attempts to put in order but remains a classification in the physiology of the mind.

The head is art—the palpable shape of our lives presented in the only way which as sensible creatures we are capable of making it objective.

The flight of Lindbergh from New York to Paris is capable of being considered in the largest possibility of its significance only as a creation of art. It is a choice under which category we approach it. It presents our spirit—the shape, that is, which our lives assume. But it is most important for us so to present it. In the broadest sense all activities of men may be so considered (the scientific and philosophic as well,—in which they finally—as far as we can tell—must gain their final evaluation,—an internal relational parallelism running horizontal in every category whether it be pure action, religious hypothesis).

Among them the most articulate of the arts is writing, whose summit is poetry. So flying is writing and Lindbergh's flight a poem: this for example.

A further example indicative of the body of knowledge, its characteristics we are neglecting, and the prejudice of our minds: Notable English men and women come to the United States, let us say, writers, since it is of writers I wish now to speak, on raids for the sale of their books, in which attack is a characteristic mode: When Mr. W. Lewis says of a poet, E. P., etc., it has the appearance of a formidable indictment.

But without respect to its truth, considering it as a statement which may not be supportable by logic, we are inclined by the habit of our thoughts to favor its *appearance* rather than to consult the body of the poems, with which Mr. [Pound] can only oppose it.

We are not capable perhaps of recognizing and judging of poetic reasons—elemental though they may be—but we do recognize and are willing to accept the scientific and philosophic appearance of what we take to be "plain" statement—which may however be entirely outside the category under discussion.

And so when I say science is a lie, philosophy a sham— the modern mental tendency is to find such a statement preposterous, strained, grossly inaccurate on the surface of it— though I make it, in a sense, the central theme of my attack.

For it is obvious that science is the very antithesis of lies— every hyphen must be proven true: it seems the one basis, the very term for accuracy—ignoring the poetic statement of Ibsen that every truth becomes a lie in 20 years. And based on this the statement of Thomas Jefferson that a revolution every 20 years is the sole guarantee of a free state. The truth of science within itself, be it scientific, in the absolute, pure sense cannot be questioned save from within by better scientific knowledge. There is no antithesis there. Lie it can only be relationally in its contact as a whole with other categories, when it tries, or by human vagary or inertia, is used out of its category to give meaning to phenomena to which it is not related: when it becomes a fetish, a catch-all, when it seeks to be absolute.

Of Philosophy, that it is a sham, as much would be granted.

But "man" implies terms and categories outside the realm of these two.

I re-assert, then, my detestation of these categories—which are resorts of escape for inadequate artists—usurping the field of vision, have become more lying as they progress, since they exclude more and more. And I re-assert that the prejudice against attack is evidence of the degree of superstition and fetishism to which the modern era has progressed since the 11th century—as selected by Henry Adams for distinction.

It should be amazing. For both philosophy and science set out with designs on a solution of life and cannot become realizable as categories of thought until they renounce those early mistaken, transcendental starts and limit themselves to being departments of function in man.

A further realm, outside, being that of art—neglected—

Not that the processes of science and philosophy are not susceptible of treatment from the viewpoint of a different body of knowledge, just as art is susceptible of scientific and philosophic treatment—and the modes of art may be used in their effects, but neither should be or can be fused with the other: The common body is man.

Obviously there is no tolerance for sham or lies in either science or philosophy. But within the category of each there is the same congruence as the infinitely more sensitive relationships of great art—in which only does the time element enter, in that the same truth in art must be restated continually in each age in the materials of that age to be true: whereas the crudity and grossness of both philosophy and science is that they attempt to do away with time in an absurd absolute which—by the very lack of time makes them—to say the least inhuman.

It is when they are related to what is beyond them that the faults appear. Until both science and philosophy, a part in the whole, renounce their transcendental pretensions and actively, themselves, combat their fetishism and relate themselves to the other categories, horizontally, in the general body of man—they are false.

There has never yet been an era when art has been the predominant category of knowledge. The artistic has been important in the great periods but incidentally. Were it to achieve the force of ascendancy—as it must finally due to finer adaptability for human use than cruder earlier divisions of understanding—a way would be opened for an entire change in the aspect of human life.

"Nothing can be done without preconceived ideas, only there must be wisdom not to accept their deductions beyond what experiments confirm." Pasteur.

April 19, 1929

Now Monaco you can't get fresh, I got a son to protect me.

Whaddaya know?
Not much. Save your money. Two soft boiled, fry two.
What?
Two soft boiled, fry two.
Who the hell told you to give orders?

[Goethe and Shakespeare]

ALL YOUNG BUCKS, laborers, thieves, blackguards, prime ministers, generals, have often a saving grace about them which is the same "looseness" in the face of the world. The thing that Goethe never saw, save at detached moments of perception, of poetry—his poems—at the moments of his poetry. (He did not follow up the philosophy of the poetry, but leaving poetry still turned to philosophy—which Shakespeare never did). Shakespeare denser, his life solely, inevitably "stupid," whereas Goethe, between poems, was intent on philosophy and being a scientific, all-round man. Shakespeare, ignorant, was living of the same substance of poetry itself which was science, philosophy, man of the world—the Faustian soul, yearning to accede to something else was not Shakespeare who lived at once fully in his "limited individuality," soundly. Champion athlete, aristocratic scion, have the character of this disreputable advance.

The New World

It is the old, continually covered out of fear of it, that is always, continually trying in the affronted consciousness of men, especially the young, to break through to an assertion. It is the expectation of this which constitutes the aspirations of each generation. It is the character of the failure which gives each age its contour. But this is actual, a cleanliness, a bareness, this Doric—

After a lifetime batting the air it is time now for me to get to work on the construction that will unite those parts in a whole.

Write of things not in derogatory or laudatory criticism —but for what they are (as the nunnery) with respect to the perception I have of them: the general scheme: the actual theme.

The New World: the sum. Floss to keep a file and an index and make it *a* complete trial for achievement and thrust for escape from my present *life after my own method.*

The New World: Note: the novel to be to demonstrate in the *low* of the environment indicated what I mean, when the elucidation-demonstration is complete (tragic or as it may be but complete—in the character of the medium, the woman, etc.), the novel is finished. The last point is the end of the novel: the character of the woman and the effect culminate. The whole contains—under the general head—in separate chapters (Shakespeare) all I have to say. First chapter, Mother with reproductions, Grandma, Pop. West Indies. The mystery. Hurrard. Statement of the records. No *right* names. Anecdotes, etc.

April 19, 1929.

(trees) "they do not even guess—not know the fury that beats about their heads" we feel—

JUNE 1, 1929
Notes:

As they leave superstition behind they (Science and Philosophy, etc.) approach the conditions of art of which, in reality, they are particular departments. To reverse the order, when they forsake the conditions of art or of being arts and seek ends apart from themselves which they deem "practical" and for that reason worthwhile they become superstitions, definable no longer in terms which are scientific and philosophical but in terms of the emotions, hope, aspiration—the prerogatives of another category of thought, inapplicable to Science and Philosophy.

The disillusion, the hopelessness which are the other facets of illusion and aspiration and which science and philosophy have latterly induced, the terrific certainties relative to human downfall and unadaptability and final annihilation with the characteristic prediction or guess that, let us say, white ants may easily supersede the human race—is a by-effect of the overemphasis, and continual hope that has been stuccoed upon Science and Philosophy by thought. Too much was desired, the illusion was too strong in the "absolute" so that, inevitably, the disillusion is terrific.

The way out is not to search further in either Science or Philosophy for faulty reasoning or more reasoning. In themselves, as arts, they are positive and excellent. The way out is to separate that which does not belong to them, the emotional connotations and fusions which are just phases

92

of a confusion of category so that they (Science and Philosophy) may become pure and, at the same time, the human element, which is quite another thing, may be re-established in its own purity, unrelated to the first.

Science and Philosophy, humanly approached, are pure acts of faith, which is their chief worth. In that they escape it in the imagination, renounced it to find a way out without it: is the proof that this is so. What remains today of that primary denial is their fetish. Art is the one means of knowledge remaining which has never made such a pretense. It measures, is accurate and devotes itself to the facts.

We should employ professional readers, craftsmen to take scientific and philosophic works and make of them each in its turn as it appears ten words—which is all, if that many, with which we can possibly be concerned.

Nothing should or does permit extensions for the general use, comfort or enlightenment but the forms of art. All study otherwise necessary for logical support only subverts the intelligence by application to it, save to the expert, the specialist whose sole permit for existence is to have the means for beating back complexity to the simple ten words it is known from the first and beforehand to be.

July 2, 1929. post-prandial!

1.: The fatal illusion of learning is that the works of antiquity, the philosophies, art pieces, political schemes, have endured; whereas they exist for us merely as symbols—of that which has lived and might live again—the cause of the time-obsession which fills our lives, and of the subjection which we suffer to the colossal modern fetishes of "progress." The truth is that when no place and no age is creating, living, these things, they do not exist. What we see is the track of something which has passed.

July 3.

—that this (in Shakespeare) is the quality in literature which is its basis—vaguely but surely apprehended (not perceived). But that it has not been accepted or noticed—

(ALL MY LIFE one thing—to break through to a more comprehensive basis away from rule—so all my work is a unit to be "formed" by perceiving this thing which is growing out of it, its full significance which, moreover, relates it to the work of my age and elevates the work of my age to a level with greatest work of other ages) for it has been feared. It negates too much, too much that is scholarly, and being basic and so dangerous (to superficiality and facile order) and difficult—in the effort to find *something* that was at least measurable *this*—immeasurable in many ways because too broad and deep—was neglected. Then to protect what has been already measured from chaos and subversion—the flat inadequate literary standard (Terrible to be inwardly convinced and not to be able to make a sweeping clarity of it destroy [the] unable and enthroned—stupidly entrenched—opposition, and to know they are right since that which is not clearly expressed *cannot* be effective—and that the function is to conserve tradition, to link life up, to hold firm. Terrible nevertheless when the wordless, emotional certainty wells up and obsesses one—driving off friends and brothers—parents and perhaps women—sometimes a whole youth of delight. It is tyrannic, obsessing—mandatory—and nothing emerges.) of today—this has been fled from as the destruction instead of the creation behind all that—a thing than can be realized—if not more.

[Shakespeare] "the man"—"Humanity" be damned—he is anonymous (nearly) and will remain so, thank God. It is the right placing of value on an ascertainable round basis of writing, to blast a stupid unenlightened makeshift of "literature" as a yardstick, that we are after—break out of bounds (Out of Bounds)take up the ball and run with it. That is what we seek to lay bare—meanwhile show the work of men who in some slight measure at least are aware of this. Not "explain" them, Christ! but distinguish their work to the exclusion of *all* work measured by the usual standard. A literary essay is intended but in a manner unprecedented —not the consecutive step by step logic but a single break through—as of troops through a line of entrenchments— single but more disordered (apparently) a much more dis- ordered-appearing progress—measured only by what we say—to the establishment (of an advanced position) of work by this good—and make a world for it.

(and tiresome, depressing to engage in arguments with "younger" men whose first lust is to ignore everything sur- rounding them and be logical, learned, understanding)

This briefly is the thesis. Little intelligence in money is another. And can we get the work, a third. It cannot be asked for gratis and it cannot be paid for since there is no money. A comment alongside their work (as in *Spring and All*), seldom directly at it.

—of which (larger view) the best *modern* writers in all languages (all the other arts) are a part, by that a unit, and by that *only*—but unrecognized since the old literature— now a phobia against them—cannot permit it until a greater basis is discovered and presented when they (that) will automatically melt. They, the moderns, are legislated *against* by stupidity, outlawed since *not* what they never intended to be. This to *include* them: to correlate if possible—, as parts of a surge into a new position, consolidated. (I have always considered myself as the *rear*-guard of the advance)

life, is so hedged round (officially) with its prohibitions, its fetishes, its don'ts, its bibles, commandments, rules of conduct, its "laws," its Rabelais only to be amused—and not

its prescient Rabelais "do as you please"—and discover laws
in operation, not on paper or in codes and literature (has
reflected) reflects this in its "grammars." If then literature
can break up into a more masterful position (above that
occupied by life) it could lead life from some modicum of
bondage to fetishes and therefore stupidities. No art for
art but *this* would be of its essence—the wholeness and
wholesomeness that Lawrence faultily presents in all his
work and in a recent poem, "The Circus," the round as
against the flat [Shakespeare] a certain roundness, a "life-
likeness" the same probably in Homer and to a less extent
Dante—not at all "literary" in any known sense but an
essence apprehended but not gauged or lucidly perceived.

Here again it enters as "lifelike," his characters taking on
a wholeness which no one has perceived to be wholly un-
literary in any accepted sense but the antithesis of—rule—

—they do not take into consideration—even tentatively—
that Shakespeare (as well as Homer) is in the classroom an
anomaly—except as he is completely passé, dead.

—in any case, to make a world without philosophy and
rejecting science—is my scheme.

Reject completely literary criteria of work—false—and
embrace a tri-dimensional one of inclusion—in which "liter-
ary"—not: everything that has been said: not "the man" but
you can't criticize a book by "rules": and to find and dem-
onstrate why some is good and some "literary good" is
rejected because dead.

Why? because there is a quality which is the essence of
what is good, which literary values do not measure—whereas
the very death of excellence measured by the "rule" is every
day rated highly. (When a thing has died, in the sense of
Eliot's *Waste Land*—or whatever it may be, and this death
is identified with the spring of literature itself—it will be
found that the death has not been properly designated, that

it has been the death of something unsuspected—and that a man of that sort of perception will turn to traditionalism, taking the death as their material.)

Beginning: Nothing less is intended than a revloution in thought with writing as the fulcrum, by means of which—and the accidental place, any place, therefore America—one like another, therefore where we happen to be, our locality, as base.

(from R) By reading this poetry, by following these precepts, by patterning our lives after these schemes—we get nothing whatever of the actuality which caused them—but a simulacrum—whose first and cataclysmic quality is that it is purely a reflection unconcerned with our reality in any way.

In any way, that is, but a gall (?) perhaps to youth who must be subject to it to drive them forward.—

[*Shakespeare*]

(CONT.) Shakespeare did not "know" the things he put down in writing (he did not have to "know" them): it would have been such an inconceivable lie (had this been so) for him to laboriously copy his knowledge out—that no man could spend a life maintaining it: a life of 34 dramas—written over a period of forty years. He lived, visibly, on the page, a vivid reality of apprehension. The knowledge came up in that form—No scholar, they are not that *kind* of objects, his words. His words would show that character of copying after a something, *in the mind of the scholar*, much more real, that is knowledge itself. They would be dead. But his words are lived particles—the antithesis of the scholarly which is the simulacrum of which I speak. His words *are* knowledge in themselves.

Shakespeare is unique, in my opinion, in this.

A typical English character which is a force, as in Elizabeth, Drake—an empiricism—a muddle (under certain aspects) but of actuality—a world bred of an island.

Shakespeare is the prime example within my measuring—and inasmuch as he, nearly anonymous, is the "mystery" of writing, and must be ingeniously explained as—an avocation of an aristocrat—so he remains the unsolved vessel of the clarification I seek.

The "good" of Shakespeare is *not* to be discovered by literary measurements—It is perceived by an anonymous sense, collective, not scholarly and so holds its mystery—as of that. Elements enter into its greatness from sources

which, though, can be more fully realized if the false
scantling of the classroom is removed.

I.

The secret of the vitality of Shakespearian characters is
that the writing does not seem to be about the characters
—but it is, in effect, the mouth of the character when in all
he says is saying always the same thing himself. In all the
characters *this* is the same since Shakespeare is no one. He
must have done this, to do it invariably, man or woman,
king or fool, by a tyrannical necessity over which he had
no power. He did it to be.

What kind of man could this have been and what kind
only? One who lived *only* by this means. One then who was
not himself outside of the character, who could not be. Not
a fool but a fluid—something quite undistinguished hunger-
ing for distinction, by no chance whatever a great savant.

It is impossible that Shakespeare could so voluntarily
annihilate himself and *be* in the characters *always* the actual:
that is, nothing besides the character. He was a homeless,
sexless-original less minded that, being almost without edu-
cation of any kind, but of large size and heady flow, took
on, in a mould that solely suited it and came ready, the only
thing it could, the actual shape of lives.

The dynamics of his dramas cannot be studied otherwise
than in the same way: as happenings. They cannot be re-
duced to a grammar if they are to be intelligently appre-
ciated. They must be approached as the effects of change in
the characters. They mean no more.

Shakespeare is misunderstood if he is made a great figure,
a bighead, a colossus of learning.—He is the effect of a kind
of thing which has been unique in the world, a namelessness
of unprecedented freedom, permeable and bulk—a dumbness
as of a tree, river, sky, nation, peasant—recording almost
mindlessly, greatness.

Mind he had (superlatively) of the keenest to get, but
to do—nothing—but reproduce without warping and with-

out distortion, prejudice—exactly what it saw: A man without other means: but terrific necessity: in that way mindless, selfless—

Scholarship has been incapable of appraising Shakespeare —or at the least has not succeeded—since he is out of its range below it.

His work may be designated as unique in excellence without the possibility of saying why—but for this or that noteworthy matter.

But its distinction is that it is unique due to a force which by itself is unrecognized in ordinary scholarship—and cannot be appraised except by first knowing the unusual cause to which it was due.

It is much more due to the present than to a timeless scholarship which thus—beats about the bush to "explain" Shakespeare by discovered rules rather than to set a new rule—or at least something outside itself, a new unscholarly kind of force, a category which in its excellence has surpassed the highest excellence of that scholarly type of mind to comprehend.

Shakespeare's plays are a new thing still in the world. They indicate a kind of knowledge of baffling identity.

Excessively imaginative, in fact, the imagination. Perhaps it is an atavism, a primitive recrudescence in an unformed age. More probably a way to *know* differently.

February 27 (Shakespeare continued) noon.

You will not discover it by examining the work directly —for evidence of existing rule. The active principle, recognized as pleasure, which is surprise, continued surprise by a force outside the understanding which satisfied the interest by supplying that for which it is waiting, teases the interest —evaporates. It is only discoverable (aside from pleasure) by approach from outside (as useful progress in chemistry follows the hypothesis and does not precede it), by ascertaining a new condition, of which only *then*, can this be discovered (verified) as an evidence. (The qualities in Shakespeare are not of course *invented* by a new hypothesis, but identified by a means which elucidates them.) I doubt very much if arguing from the work the condition, which is a living state of the imagination, superior to any of the parts of high scholarship is one, could be arrived at.

He played the ghost.

To make of such a man and his works a convention is to present scholarship in the worst light, succinctly an imperative chuckle-headedness which amounts to a retreat before experience, a defect of orientation (to explain Villon amounts to the same) which is fundamental in it so that all its arguments are limited and distorted by this defect of the premise.

It is another element of activity which is major to life and by the lack of which scholarship is permitted to exist. But proper scholarship should and does (rarely) take into consideration that it is, so to speak, stopping the film to study it. And that thereby it loses something, this principle of activity—which in men of the cast of Shakespeare and Villon, of actuality, is their relieving and most powerful element. It is something else, added to understanding.

A man whose rigid limitation of applicability of understanding released him (as scholarship is released by its static narrowness) unprecedentedly to run over the whole field of observable fact without straying, a whole life spent in the doing of a single, unvariable thing—and nothing else to be remembered by.

He can be understood solely imaginatively (an English trait I am sure—where Latin lucidity is unknown) from the category, or viewpoint, of the imagination. That is, seized whole *first*, as a new or rarely indicative species, *then* attacked, subserviently by the science, since it is purely and limitedly that, of literary scholarship—in *that* (foreign—unable fully) category.

Deducing from the whole what kind of man: strange to his time and to his family. Typical of the stage to the world at large. Questioned at home, unquestioned elsewhere. But far more at home in that which he seemed least.

.

JULY 7.

1.

Afraid lest he be caught in a net of words, tripped up,
bewildered and so defeated—thrown aside—a man hesitates
to write down his innermost convictions. Especially is this
true after forty when all his life has formed, perhaps into
a single strand which allows him to say to himself that life
is to him a reasonable thing, of related parts coordinated
and workable—no matter what the end. If this be lost, this
certainty which must pass for hope, this comforting inward
sense of his own personal integrity lost in a crashing to-
gether of words which will not be resolved into lucidity—
the lucidity he feels in his whole being somewhere—it is the
end. He fears.

It cannot be that this certainty which alone carries him
forward is false. Rarely does he think of that. Yet might it
not be that to be too explicit—in words—might blast his
comfort, this solidity of his mind? To write it down might
prove his feelings just that, feelings alone, in themselves
nothing, a fool's paradise of self-deception in which he
manages to hide himself somehow in order to live at all.
Better to leave it so. Where ignorance is bliss 'tis folly to be
wise.

But it is just this which drives a man on. For how can he
be certain that his conviction, which if it be worth anything
at all (must be able to bear examination) is so, unless he
test it explicitly by statement? It must be written down, bit
by bit, as he may, in fear for his lack of skill at words,

watching them, distrusting them—yet counting on them to help him, to bring what he knows he must believe into a searchlight of scrutiny. And who knows, it may be that he will succeed. If so his life will be strengthened, placed on a higher level of purity, made into the thing he admires more than anything else: the understanding of himself which he imagines many men possess in the world.

Therefore he writes, attempting to strike straight to the core of his inner self, by words. By words which have been used time without end by other men for the same purpose, words worn smooth, greasy with the thumbing and fingering of others. For him they must be fresh too, fresh as anything he knows—as fresh as morning light, repeated every day the year around.

Why not avoid writing and read? For the wisdom of the ages is inaccessible. Mountains of dead words, cemeteries of words befog the mind. Now another book. It cannot be helped. The conviction that fills the whole body of a man is nearer to him than all the books that have ever been written. And these other books, the great philosophies, the endless treatises of science, the books of religions and the lives of other men—the biographies, the histories—what are they? They are part of the very oppressive, stupid, aimless, ignorant world which has driven him to shelter, to prison within himself, to defeat from which he must escape. HE must escape, weak, comparatively unlettered, by himself. Then, when he is whole and only then will the wisdom of the ages be decipherable.

If he has written poetry it may help. He knows at least something of the difficulties of form. Style he takes to be a word like the others. It is all one thing. To say what must be said; to say it once that it may blossom once like a hollyhock or a bird—then let it begin to die—even while he himself is alive he will see his own writing grow older and begin to die. He may live to see it completely dead. But that is no reason for halting. It is in fact the beginning he wants. Write that it may become clear—if possible, to escape ignorance and confusion. By seeing his own words die while he goes on living he will learn to estimate the value of the classics.

In the classics something seems to him—to the world—hard and to endure. But what is it that endures? It is nothing but himself, but his own desire to be clear, to know, to coordinate, to undertand. The classics, the sayings, the elucidations, are dead as shells, as fossils of plants which can still be studied in fine tissue-paper-thin flakes under the microscope, the very prehistoric plant cells still visible so that species can be determined and varieties named. These things represent men who lived and felt the desire to write just as he does, who wrote fresh from the whole body and who went on living after. Something hard has remained. It is desire. To live cannot be learned from the writings of others. It is the life of writing that comes from inside. The classics prove it.

Write. It is surely a deed, as much as digging or a gift to a comrade or a beggar. All one needs learn from the past is that it existed and not to try to convince. It must be put down each for himself, read each for himself. If it is there it will be gathered—or not. It is in that like fruit on a tree, each will use it or not as he wills. It is—in that it is wholly for himself, to himself—impersonal the only impersonal. It is for that—perhaps—another might reject writing, even reject reading quite justifiably and need feel no shame, no compunction, no lack. It is not necessary to read. It is not necessary to write. One may do as one pleases. It may be that cutting wheat gives everything that can be achieved by the arts, all of them, in a rough way, or even dissipation. But one *may* write as well as do anything else that can be named. One *may* read.

If one writes it will be, then, like the classics, of an inner conviction common to all men of his existence, to make it comprehensible, or more comprehensible—as another might do it with his hands alone.

And there is still another reason besides mere rebellion

why one should want to write and not merely read. It is that there is an antagonism between the ages. Each age wishes to enslave the others. Each wishes to succeed. It is very human and completely understandable. It is not even a wish. It is an inevitability. If we read alone we are somehow convinced that we are not quite alive, that we are less than they—who lived before us. It grows and obsesses us. It becomes a philosophy, a cynicism. We feel that something has died but we are not quite sure what. Finally it seems to be the world, the civilization in which we live. Actually we are enslaved. It is necessary to overcome that.

And the difficulty is all with words. With worn and broken words we are trying to do the same that men with new, sharp-edged words have done before. That is why the best minds of our century—some of them—are bent first on inventing a new language—and how they are hated for it. But the difficulty is all one of words. The classics have done something to the words. They have fixed them into an apparent building which can do nothing but crumble and disappear like the Parthenon. All that can be said has been said there—but it is crumbling away. But in among the structures of words—though the aging and breaking is more subtle—it is going on just the same. Fixed in words—in the very classics are many—most—if not all of the stupidities which enthrall us, which make us want to write, which inspire us to break out. To read, while we are imbibing the wisdom of the ages, we are at the same time imbibing the death and the imbecility, the enslaving rudeness of the ages.

WE are the center of the writing, each man for himself but at the same time each man for his own age first. But his battle is with the words, the difficult words which he must approach fearfully. The difficulties being two: within himself—if what he would say exists at all and—with the words, whether they can be found at all and used to match this reality which is there—he is sure—unmatched throughout the ages—the one thing in the classics translatable.

July 4 (copied from Rx blanks) old–

There are bodies that are like iron. We speak of courage but the fragile back that crumbles under a shock is a poor support for it. Not that a man need be heavy. A small hard man you cannot break is one of the most resistant. Daniel Boone was stocky, tough, middle height. A descendant of his is the same. The Scotch during the war were hardest to break, go about two weeks in the ranks with 3 or 4 pieces of shrapnel in the calf of the leg, saying nothing. It is the weak body precedes often the timid mind—unless it give the mind a new direction.—The nerves also play a part. Bat Nelson was anesthetic over his skin surface. Children, babies show it. Some are painfully surfaced, some have no terminal nerves at all. It might be shown under the microscope. Teeth show it. Some suffer agonies. In childbirth women vary. And the mind may be of all sorts to go with it. Financiers are often brute types with acute senses, sensual.

(The Descent of Winter) Darker and darker grows the scene with lovelock in all trees—absence and snow—

July 12, 1929.

I dedicate all that I have lost and never wanted—

Hysteria is due to suggestibility and dissociation of personality. Charcot.

The nature of the body can only be understood as a whole.— Hippocrates (Horsehead)

108

The subtlists—like G. B. S.—act on the belief that men have missed the truth (and this is their truth which they build all their hopes upon) by stupidity, maladjustment, flaw in vision and ratiocination. And thus, they, by wit, smartness, adjustment (small) giving a surface of brightness, can gain truth by exercise of cleverness; not realizing that they along with those they believe they supersede—are all in a colossal and crude impasse which they do not see (all being by that of one kind only, their subtleties quite accidental) and but scratches the surface.

"Philosophy"—is today no more a knowledge of man than it is crap—see Hippocrates on the body (above) [p. 108]. It is experimental psychology. But if one man (a whole) can simply but comprehensively coordinate his life—another can do the same. But simply—that it reaches, not *may* reach, the least individual who is granted to be *like* all others (this is the basis of Christianity). Thus the least is a measure since *all* are at least that. The more complex never being a measure since they surpass the least who remain, to that degree, outside the category. The mistake has been to grow sentimental and to confuse least with lowness, a pure coincidence. Today nobody is coordinated, philosophers least of all.

Catholicism (a religion) offers intellectual integrity (when the basic axiom has been granted) but at the cost of the intelligence (since the tranquilizing tenet cannot be accepted). It is all argument out of "God's" hat. The same error is committed here as by science: to ignore the basis which exists—the Shakespearian *man*. But accepted (Catholicism) offers a (scholastic) "explanation" of trees, earth, morals, bees—the various St. Thomases, St. Anthonies, St. Francises—a very old, very beautiful and influential whole: the original and unacceptable postulate.

The body (Rabelais) distressful perhaps, the Adam and Eve, is avoided—left to literature, profane writing: the pagan thrust that is—Shakespeare.

An Essay on William Shakespeare:
My Grandfather

HERE (in S) knowledge was used in a different form, not at all as Lord [Bacon] used it. Very well, it can be answered that B possessed knowledge to such a degree that he also possessed the knowledge (and the ability) to disconnect it from the academic, the didactic, the simply deductive. Good, then it is of little account whether you call him S or B. He is in that mood the Shakespeare of whom I speak, completely (but without a trace) divorced from knowledge as explanation, and at work on knowledge as colored stones. It is, in Shakespeare, a juxtaposition of and interaction between pieces (when not sentimental of the time with "humor") and not a qualitative, quantitative chemistry.

(Later in A. M.) The artist as opposed to the scientist—the opaque artist in whom, in whose work, the world, life holds or is held as opposed to the lucid scientist through whom, whose work, everything passes, is in a flux, unheld, a pure time matter—as opposed to the artists themselves (in this way the artist and the religious are opposed to science —but artists are mainly—unfortunately stupid—they have that unfortunate predilection due to their kind—that they are stuck on something, the religious on "God," the artist on a world of sticks, and philosophers, religionists and scientists with all the particles they tray out and mull over); his [the scientist's] spatial location, whose last analysis leads just to—pure motion—the immaterial (he who though he was searching to the absolute material) (before his eyes), the electron. Two opposed processes—nowhere else seen in Bacon's work.

Shakespeare could be all he is and at the same time—completely without a knowledge of "nature" as a cause. He could be ignorant, unschooled and no thinker—in the sense of a disrupter, an analyser, an iconoclast which at basis Bacon surely was. In fact given a mind and no lust whatever for causes he would be just the one to be set spinning about an opaque interior (like the earth) elaborating timelessly his puzzlements or "knowledge," his dramas, his design. Whereas Bacon is intent on eliminating everything, opaque, to do away with the earth (intellectually). (Shakespeare, the flower of the period just before Bacon—come to an end with his advent—that is "end" in the historical sense, not that of intelligence—eclipse)—the end result of Science, which he started, being that it *is* done away with (its own materials)—nothing opaque at all, but a manifestation of pure time—a motion. (chemistry and physics: one.)

Shakespeare's way stopped with him, the spatial, the timeless (no more mediaeval than Greek), positively not mediaeval, but the scientific was bound to come out of the Renaissance, it is in its essence religious. The Shakespeare is much more further back and it is an archaism to us (very much alive)—it has been left behind (in the mind—not in adherence—surrounded with nostalgia, the nostalgia of kings Shakespeare himself senses), and is used only by the very ignorant (those that religion gathers up pebblewise to cement into the walls of its cathedrals without changing them—the human pebble!).—No man of genius could very well attempt it in a scientific millennium. Shakespeare could since he was accidentally gifted with brain but no classic.

The classic (Renaissance etc.) by some chance of his life (insular) didn't occur. Too late (fortunately) he sought it but it only colored with names like Caesar, Cleopatra, etc.—never a philosopher in any of Shakespeare's pieces—only men and women of action—bent by what you will—something more solid which was there *before*, something he could not escape, opaque, unscientific, in an awakening scientific era, which Bacon was first in awakening. Shakespeare had nothing but people to oppose to that, a solid rock he could not break—just arrange, rearrange. He *could* not get by them. There he stuck and spun.

Gui. Is he at home?
Bel. He went hence even now.

There's the solidity, the mystery, the fullness of Shakespeare. The "he" is solid, admits no question, is full of boding and—momentarily for Shakespeare—full of change, tragedy: free though of theory, of postulate of—like religion —like "god." It is the solidity of—what is best to the moderns.

Naturally, the modern is not trying or wishing or dreaming to bring back Shakespeare: it is however in great measure a revolt against the two great fetishes of life, "science" and "philosophy." It has no objection to the processes of science and philosophy but refuses their conclusions to embrace anything, it sides with religion in that—but puts that in its category, its god-category, admiring its intelligent symbolism in the Thomasian sense. And strangely, finds the work of Shakespeare tremendously illuminating. His pessimism is plainly of no matter, his conclusions are nil, his "philosophy" and "knowledge" void, of no serious pretense. But his solidity, his opacity is growing familiar. The twaddle over Hamlet is an incident, or better, it is the place where the Hamletian condition which Shakespeare found himself in in a dawning scientific age shows most clearly. It is a symptom of Shakespeare's intelligent position in his world—it is not at all the matter of his writing. This could be strung out into fine strands to no purpose.

(RETRO—things that were in my portfolio)

—a luminous conviction that but for the stupidity men ex-
hibit—the major of which are their adherence through a
subtle senility to the concepts of science, philosophy, history
—they would, by pure negative—by the removal of impedi-
ments, arrive at renewals.

Not to remove the *benefits* of science. It is the imagination
that offers and would suffer the change.

It is to step up out of a less mobile category of which
science is a type, from a fetishism with history, to a force
which, saving the effects of science, could use them minus
their gratuitous effects on the intelligence.

At the beginning of the century a child could see that
as a major occupation of the intelligence science was fin-
ished. At such a time multiplication of services takes the
place of serious effort, and the type of genius represented
by Thomas Edison is predominant, the theories of "service"
(not the fact), the pragmatism, and philosophical (cinemati-
zations) (slow motion) amateurs were turned up. An effort
made to stem the inevitable flux which was taking place—
odd figures here and there: the Pounds. A tentative search
for a new is all that a man could use. Red blood, action,
Empire—due apparently to local causes but related to the
state of the intelligence finally.—Science was at an end and a
man's occupation with being, which is his sole major con-
cern, must take its place—machines, yes, but as a subsidiary
to a deeper reality lost to science completely: the American
thing.

113

America must have impressed a man especially one living here unconcerned with the small temporary problems, science, history, philosophy presenting so many fragments capable of infinite subdivisions with which Wundt, or any anatomist might be concerned—Freud with the palpably unimportant expedient of sex—art presented a scope, seriousness in a degree neglected.

We marvel at the masterpieces of Holbein, of Rembrandt or even at the older daguerreotypes. We wish for a similar vitality of touch in modern work. But it does not occur to us that faces do not exist to that degree of intensity today. The people pass totally blank, not even possessed by minds not their own—a mindlessness, a blank. How to paint them? Not. The vitality (which then existed in faces) is in other phases of the pictorial art (since it is that under discussion). But the emptiness remains.

The first difficulty of modern life is a difficulty of thought; not emphatically, of philosophy nor of philosophic thinking—but of thought, of the imagination of the world, the immediate. The philosophy of it is a category, under the general head.

—most difficulties of thought rest upon the basis that the purest intelligence can never become official. Either the power is lacking to the ability or the ability is lacking to the power. It is a general principle of natural economy to insure the slow progress necessary to biologic safety—be damned. But it must at the same time be observed that it causes wreckage in the advance members who must always be unsupported until proven—and their work is taken over by a secondary brand of less sensitive organization—

Things called scientific information or facts or elucidations; philosophic truths, historic verifications—constitute the world of make-believe, of evasion, in which we live. The world waits for immediacy, Villon, Shakespeare, that is their significance as against the postponements of the "heavens." Li Po's immediate love of the Moon is wisdom.

The Refinement

SIMULTANEOUSLY eliminate the waste to refine the one ele-
ment desired—Pasteur noted. They (the works under the old
system—the lawful) do not exist, not from ineptitude but
because they do not contain that *one* thing. That element
because of which *alone* the good is good. That rare refine-
ment of action that cannot be taught—but is in all categories
when it lusts—Villon, Sappho, etc.—which they have been
missing, and lacking which—a *perception*—all their crude
(well made) organizations are lying failures.

This has always been the basis of art and the simple diffi-
culty of understanding between the artist and his world. It
is that of an unrelated category trying to envision in its
terms a principle which governs it along with a number of
similar . . . It is the basis for the unutilized viewpoint of the
artists in general affairs—a severe check to the artist and a
loss to the world which resists that which would throw the
reigning category into the subservient second place destined
for them—as Freud. It is obvious to all that sex is a matter
of no importance in itself; a means. Freud denies all this.

—for example from this basic point of view of the artist,
work in the various categories of the intelligence takes on
certain discrete circumscribed shapes (like a bucket or any
other *object*—which they are) with internal relationship
important to that category only (and so semblable to works
of art to an artist), thus in history the downfall—Freud,
England and its politics—these became whole, simple, under-
standable and nonobsessive—a relief takes the place of the
hypnotism of too close application.

These results of Science and Philosophy are thus found

to be not "true" but only when considered in relationship to the category. Thus all need very much correcting and are valuable principally (to themselves) as criticism of the special category, say of history itself. In a larger sense, that of art, they may be and at times as at present, are lying.

Release whole areas of feeling accessible to them (Science and Philosophy, etc.) by and because of limitation to a small, protected field. They are precisely like walled cities but the artist who has been the brigand has and always had this degree of justice on his side that he went between and lived openly. In life a man chooses a profession—the most onerous moment to the growing intelligence since it signifies truly—amputation. Later (in the category) the man visualizes a type of freedom but is sad since he knows instinctively it is only a simulacrum. Certain men keep the real and are called vagrants. It is of them the real interest speaks—

There is a choice, a polarity in the arts which presents itself to the intelligence for allegiance one way or the other. It is the same that exists in chemistry, life at large or whatever it may be. It is the "pure" as opposed to the "practical." Pure chemistry as opposed to industrial chemistry. A nun (or a prostitute—phases of one thing) as opposed to a wife. It is the school of applied design at one pole and—the artist.

A boy whose father has been a hard working and fairly successful physician studies medicine and decides to embrace the field of investigation in comparative anatomy. The Skeleton of the times: Stein.

These are simple distinctions involving no emotion or tendency to recrimination. There are these choices and men make them, one is right, one is left. When a science or an art is at its period of greatness the "pure" phase of it must have preceded its application to the opportunity of the moment. There is no need to say which is the better of the two, merely that the two exist. Or certainly without pure distinction, as an art or a branch of thought in whatever form, it lags and is superseded by something else where the tendency to rush to a pure distinction is more marked. And where that thrust occurs that place will be marked as the scene of greatness.

In painting, the pure is design. It is painting itself. For a hundred years in France it has been predominant. It has uncovered endless "means" "borrowed" by industrial art. But art itself exists distinct from that. It is not a dray horse carrying something for an alien purpose.

Writing has never been observed as so clearly polarized. The times today are particularly offensive to any realization of such a condition. It is a mistake to speak of experimental writing. The distinction is not deep enough. There is pure writing and writing which is made to be the horse of any one who has a burden to carry. All this is obvious and is simple and should be observed with some interest in an intelligent community.

Failure to recognize it, violence to oppose, are however the marks of the times. Writing as an art is of course completely inundated by journalism, which is meant to "put something over." But all other writing is more or less in the same class with journalism. It all belongs to that pole. Textbooks, plays, histories, the Shaw's, the Welles's, the endless novelists: all these things make one group. Not one of them is interested in writing save as a means to put something over.

Pure writing is represented by all whose interest is primarily in writing as an art, of far more interest to them than what it conveys. Surely there should be a place in the intelligence for them if not in the practical world. It is the lack of this primary consideration which is offensive in a place like the United States.

Naturally the hatred springs from fear. The language is the storehouse of the traditions of the people. Language is not stable. Leaks occur and—though they are clearly aware of it or not—the lives of people are modified by accidents of language. And men instinctively feel it. There is a self-preservational dread of changes of language. For after all, aside from language that is understood more or less commonly by everyone, we should soon find ourselves lost in a howling wilderness where there would be nothing "holy."

But for this very reason, if we were really an intelligent community governed by anything but fetishes, pure investigations in language and its forms should be fostered by the state.

It is impossible for any group of people to change their habits until the language has first given them the means to state their objective, this is the only permissible use of "ideals." As a "pure" art language is today preparing a kind of instrument (not for that "purpose" however) which people require for a step up into the difficulties of a nearer and more varied approach.

Is anything more stupid than international conflict? Where one wishes to bind or to murder the other—most specially in Europe for years due to the irregular coast line. But how, barring the work in painting, in writing, will forms be found to embody a better adjustment? The mind must be stepped up from arithmetic to solid geometry, at least. If this is not done nothing can take place. And pure writing will be the means.

Pasteur played around in stale beer. Not very promising material, what? He also damn near starved. He advanced "pure" bacteriology. But why oppose him? That to me is the perennial disgust with people. Why not welcome him? Why rush to condemn, to defend the realm like Wyndham Lewis? It is the purest stupidity, as an art in itself maybe. Thus Stein must be placed. Her genius is in that primarily, she has been one of the discoverers of the place where writing is to be attacked, a new plane—or as I say polarity. It is very primitive, very crude—but it is placed in the right location.

Naturally she cannot be expected to be read—yet.

It is childish and pathetic.

Another aspect, slightly rotated, of the same thing is the everlasting (modern) misunderstanding arising from the contentions, on the one hand, that art should "mean" something, and on the other, held by other more or less word-lacking radicals, that it means nothing.

This is the same old difficulty of the confusions of terms.

Certainly it means nothing, and certainly it must mean something: what?

In the crudest cases, a poem was thought to need a moral. The fork and the sense are separate. It goes on down to the present, when symbolism is refurbished for the French Academy to oppose the present "direct" writing. Symbols, then, must mean something and art the adjustment of symbols. The symbols thus become as words in a sentence and the sentence must "mean" what it says. A moral. It is all one.

To mean something means just that, a moral, a burden, a lesson, a textbook, a thought, an idea, a narration—decorated and detailed. These are the things that mark historic periods and designate the minds of the times.

But after all, these things are quite justly no part of art. They are life, philosophy, what not. Art has nothing whatever to do with them. A work of art can have, justifiably, no such meaning without doing itself violence. It has, justly, no "meaning." It is a work of art. And that, on the other hand, is precisely its significance.

There is but one burden justifiable to a work of art. That is itself—as part of a whole. It must at best, quite truly, mean nothing as the antisymbolists say. A chemical experiment or discovery fraught with terrific consequence for the world, in the moment of its conception and execution and perfection, can and does mean nothing, in the same way. The glow that suffuses the chemist, sensation with a vengeance if one must be so stupid, relates to the art of chemistry purely. Nothing may ever come of the thing any more than it may come of the amazing formulae of the differential calculus.

These things carry no symbolism, they have no meaning.

But in writing the precisely important thing is the very exposition that such things have no meaning. Stein does that. A childish jumble of pages from the dictionary doesn't do that.

—quite truly a work of art means nothing, as the anti-symbolists say. Nothing, that is, but itself. Which is of course *something*.

This is the exact point at which the present lies.

Its significance is itself, as fresh as a new leaf.

This distinction may seem academic and unimportant but if the Wayside Inn can be filled by its distinguished patron with "rare Americana" it is not difficult to see that if this same enthusiasm for locality could be translated, in the manner of a Medici, into a deeper interest, a rarer if somewhat difficult insight into the needs of "pure" art, tremendous changes might be effected.

It is a constant source of amazement to me that with all the cash there is free in America there is not one great mind with genius toward the "pure" in art to endow, or buy work of the rare few who are doing modern work. Morgan bought freely out of a conservative if rich imagination. But if he could have seen the field of art with the radical eye with which, perhaps, he saw the field of finance the result would have been to place America in an advanced position in the start superior to any.—But what of it, naturally. He didn't and couldn't.

All he could do in the end was to found collections, museums and schools—all useless.

The creative mind is jealous of wealth. It would rival a Morgan and make his field, finance, seem insignificant. These, this form the "jealousies" which defeat support. They prevent endowment of active minds in fields or categories tangent to the popularities of the moment. It is not docile, asks nothing.

Only one abstract idea has been put over strongly in the western world: Christianity. Science, nothing like as well, Philosophy, poorly. Art, never. Should it occur it would have a transforming effect incomparably greater than all the rest. It is more to the ultraviolet side of the spectrum of the categories of the intelligence. Pure, it is stripped to penetrate.

Such men (Morgan, etc.) like to feel themselves kings, as they are (in their category) and to enhance the illusion they purchase works of art, the effects of the great of the past whose crowns of light they think to borrow. But let American purchasers especially recognize that they are not even comparable, much less to the great artists but not even to the great patrons.

For the ancient patrons supported living artists, gave bed and board to present genius.

The American wealthy all turn away from the present to the past. For they sense rivalry.

The Skeleton of the Times

The various categories of the intelligence have each an individual characteristic which sharply separates it from all others. Their extension and pliability also vary. Some are narrow and bare, others are extremely extensive, even to the point of seeming to be limitless, and full of luxuriance. Science has been one of these and philosophy another. But all categories are limited.

Their history, itself a category, varies. Some have been extensively explored, some less so, some very little. And their influence on culture also has varied, whole periods being marked by the preponderance of one pilgrimage, one might almost say, through the field of some certain category of the mind.

As each new field opens thought rushes in with curious accumulations from other categories and other times. This leads to the chief errors of thought, which have resulted in the chief characteristics of the day—confusion and despair. Each category as it engages the attention is thought to be the great answer the limits of which are in Paradise. Whereas each is nothing more than a part of the whole though sharply defined from the others, much in the manner of the pagan gods—a logical arrangement much nearer to the understanding than the very vaguely defined saints of the Christian Church, each have clear attributes.

But in the pursuit of knowledge in any one category a striking thing is that the highest reaches are attained only by the strictest exclusion of the effects of every other category, the particles tend to become distinctly "pure" and more difficult to achieve. And, on the other hand, the greatest offense in any category is to include the effects of some other in gaining spurious positions of thought, thought to be strategic.

But again, obsessed with the convolutions of thought in one segment of the whole, the mind loses touch with the rest and makes the very serious error of believing it has achieved conclusions which govern the others. This is entirely idle and comes of the very primary defect of logic where two things are being confused in one solution. Philosophy has been the chief offender in this respect with its pursuit of "the Absolute" which is nothing whatever—outside of philosophy. Science has been even worse with its search for the origin of "life." Both the absolute and life belong to entirely different categories than the ones in which they are being searched for. The absolute belongs to the whole group of categories as a whole, and life to the instinctive group common to the plants and animals where science is not extant.

Yet, men believe in each category as it is brought out, exactly as they believed in dynasties and kings formerly. And as each, in the manner of Lord Bacon, sets out to conquer the world—and fails, the despair that ensues runs over into everything, indiscriminately. And the tempo of one—

The tempo of search grows faster, as in science today. That too encloses all, runs over into all categories without reason. Until a collapse occurs—due to the exhaustion of one category. Blindnesses, mistakes, confusions. Today it is the end of science. Whose unrelated conclusions are falsely applied to every situation in life whether they are alien or otherwise.

After men arouse themselves from the confusion incident upon their awakening after the collapse of fetishism in any one category—marking great periods of the world—intervals occur which mark periods of the world fairly distinctly.

It is at such times that great abstract ideas and pure knowledge reawaken and a new thrust comes on. Today when science has so far overreached its use to the mind and is being exploited laterally at ever-increasing speed, men are chiefly in despair since they have borne too heavily upon it and it is failing them.

Despair grows coincidentally with the extension of the effects of science since each extension carries with it something of the quandary in which the "pure" knowledge finds itself.

These things are usually excessively simple. But the extremely interesting point to notice is that this despair is not essential but due to a confusion, an obsession, a fetishism with the category taking the place of a divine presence in which men have been led to believe. The category is entirely neutral, a source of "purity," a thing which gets out of hand, out of perspective, and is only one of many others, each have the same relative necessities which govern it.

When one category gets into a state of confusion, as science is today, and men regret the 11th century where life was a whole—it is not an unreasonable condition but a very healthful one indicating a withdrawal from obsession and a strong desire to re-establish the mind on a sounder basis.

Despair of life is an entirely unnatural thing foisted on the mind by its confusions. There need be no embellishment or hope either. Life that has not despaired in the past need not do so now. The effects of investigation in one category, such as science, affect it not at all. But this must be rediscovered perennially.

What the next category must be cannot but be the chief concern of man. Philosophies are outdated. History is only itself, a fixed thing entirely in the past. It leads to the same confusions as science. The present thesis is a plea to the intelligence for all that is most modern in art as the only way open to the mind for a rejuvenation of life.

The Embodiment of Knowledge

THE SKELETON—further note—This is to point out again, to the intelligence, the significance of the larger category of man, and to make a special plea for the usefulness of the field of art, especially art in its modern phases.

—to outline the nature of some of the attacks upon it and their unreasonableness.

. . . until, as learning accompanied by popular adherence approaches the limits of its category (of the age), its acceleration increasing and apprehension growing of an "end," it is translated into a general—wholly unrelated despair. Life cannot be predicated from any one category.

July 31   #1

You'd think that men of intellectual distinction would sometimes notice and draw illuminating conclusions relative to the force of general ideas—apart from their own realm of proficiency, in which truly, as Dr. C. Mayo has said, they often seem to know more and more of less and less.

the origins of change, in what realm it lies—the low: a poor bastard profligate Jew. How much the general category has been instrumental above any special field in originating all endeavor.

But it is difficult to think, difficult to stay on the niceties of a thought, to remain on the general category of man and not make the mistake of falling in among the strings of the instrument.

It is especially difficult when one has been trained in the, so to speak, manners of one category such as—let us say business organization on a large scale. Men so stiffened frequently die when released.—Philosophy, science, art or what not.

For the peculiarities of any salient are learned along with thinking—and may, do, in fact must limit the ability. A philosopher, quite extraordinarily, must maim his ability to think the deeper he delves into the idiosyncracies of his special field. A thing largely ignored.

Flexibility of thought is so precious that sometimes it seems the only virtue of the mind—the only virtue the mind needs.

(end of #1)

July 31.

—under these circumstances—when thought approaches the end of each category and is drawing false conclusions of that in a *general nature*—the more subtle becomes the thought the further it is removed from the truth.

11

Under such circumstances a mind of an unusual broad shape may intervene to realign experience. Catastrophe has taken its place in the past.

What is the nature of catastrophe? The end of special categories and the scrapping of partial irregular peaks into a lower but more general level.

The unrecognized thing, as usual in large movements, has been its essential all-embracing character. But mourning for lost eminence, and inability to start again in fields inheriting disaster have followed.

The usual designation of such ages might be "humanistic."

But this is not satisfactory to thought. The real designation is—a return to the category of the whole.

This lesson can be learned by thought but it has not been as yet. Every man so far, has been misled by the childish error of searching for an "absolute" in a special category. Without exception, no one has been able to escape it. Perhaps the practicing artist has come nearest.

(this is a good size for a "chapter")

July 31 (loose, in between notes.)

—it had best be done (find the errors of allotment in any one category) by someone outside the particular category.

The errors—typically in Science and Philosophy—which have led to the present day quandary of thought (less so of life)—are childish in their simplicity.

This is the sole reason for their being missed by such highly convoluted and astute minds. And shame on the ordinary person at the presumption he would assume in calling attention to them and their primacy.

How shall the un-initiated enter the ground of trained men? It is neither permissible nor possible. The "Sacred Grove" must remain inviolate to him.

Save only as it is a part of a whole which it shares with all else. This is his, the uninitiate's sole ground.

And here he may stand. Astute minds could not miss anything more complex.

It is with misgiving that anyone can bring them out since it seems incredible, so noticeable, so used to them—that they are like the wall paper in a familiar room—never seen.

Expert though they may be in their own category, in classic literature, let us say, they may be childlike in another.

Let them learn to do the crawl. So they may be puerile in the treating of "the New Humanism"—or in predicting the outcome of a boxing match—mistaking the surface for the essential, missing sequences—just in the manner of any malapert.

One has to smile, sometimes, if one is able, at philosophers in their little cubicle of thought, ignoring—not failing to observe—but ignoring the movements of a cat in an entirely different category. Or a scientist in his laboratory, for that strictly is his confines, observing, perhaps, a fly or a stenographer through the window in the next office building; or some disguised publicist, immured by an empire waiting for some Genghis Kahn to carry dirt up behind successive charges of archers until a ramp is built and the wall mounted and that country taken.

Such things are, in truth, puerile.

First one then another of the categories comes into ascendency, a constant variation—marking the physiognomy of the ages. Poetry is one of these.

When knowledge is at a crest it is an age of enlightenment, when down we speak of the dark ages. There is no doubt a great wave of all the categories of knowledge synchronously. But there is also a relative range of shifts between them so that one may be up, another down.

It is with the place of poetry today I have to deal.

When a young astronomer asserts the superiority of his material, the stars, [to] that of the poet, words, he does this at least correctly, he objectifies the words as the material of poetry, differentiates at the same time between their use to him, an astronomer, and to another, who is a poet.

But to say that either words or stars are the material of either science or poetry, shapes perceptible to the senses— it would be better to go slow—for are they not corollaries only of the brain? Were we to scrape the words from the paper, or the stars from the sky, they would mean alike, nothing. It is only in their interrelationship with the perceptions that we know them. And there they are equally real.

In writing there are depths to be sounded as deep as any sky—as material, as full of value. Futile to say that one would hate to take words as a material, so limited—but every lexicography is full of enormous constellations, whereas poetry itself lies before us limitless.

And old science and the old poetry are very much the same—without their contemporary counterparts—helpers to the mind.

And here is the noteworthy—what good are they to us—should we stop our efforts to new modes for them—what good are they to us now?

None whatever. Vital as they were, they are no longer possessing of those materials, the stars.

Can the physics of even fifty years ago—as it existed then—be said to objectify its material as it exists now?

Poetry the same.

As said, no category of the understanding need synchronize with the other—as science had its dark ages when poetry was with the other arts at a zenith, so now when science is up, poetry is in an age of darkness.

Not that excellent work is not done during such periods. It is excellent and important in the continuous train of the work. From prestige, as its lack poetry is surely now lower than ever. But its materia cannot be destroyed any more than those of Science, since they are the same.

Science be it remembered, changes nothing, invents nothing, takes away nothing, adds nothing to the material world. How can it? It does one thing only—it brings its material into a certain relationship with the intelligence, in its relationship with man and poetry, brings man into a diagonal relationship with it.

When one shall be paramount, when the other, no one knows, nor why. It is of that interrelationship of the categories of which there is no knowledge, to which there is no approach. Unless one borrow the question entirely and say—it is man himself of which—save you split him up (which is inadmissable) we know nothing whatever.

If he die, why is it not that he is a parasitic creature, destroying as he goes and like all destroyers he is doomed. Why shall he not live upon nuts and fruit, or like certain insects and trees on decay? Then perhaps he will have found the secret.

Poetry seems a breath of life in this sense, where all the rest at their lives seem meaningless and dead beside it.

As far as man is concerned, science, poetry, philosophy—are no more than material manifestations of his brain, of equal value whether in clay, iron or words—provided only that they keep at a stretch the bounds of his comprehension.

Before any of the arguments begin they must be placed, for from place, a place, begins everything—is in fact a place. Synchronously occupied by everything and at the same time space itself—nothing but. Before science, philosophy, religion, ethics—before they can begin to function—is a region unsusceptible to argument. It is not the past, whose sole property is place.

Here lies the un-human, call it what pleases, super, per, sub. It is only (if at all) accidentally in the past for the intelligence—but that gives it objectivity. We have not progressed out of it (the past) for it is here now exactly as it was then. It cannot be called the "unknowable," the superhuman before which we plead ignorance—for how have we data to say that? It is simply the unlogical, including all our past, (our past fits into it, not it into our past)—they are not the same. It is this that may be apprehended only.

The Importance of Place

> "Chaque figure repose et s'ap-
> perie sur son ombre." *Journal
> des Faux-Monnayeurs.*

THE CHARACTER area of myths, of which the past of human history consists—and upon which rests all his later knowledge, the immaterial ultimate reality guessed at by philosophers, the religious heaven and hell (projections of the same)—all that is outside of deduction, and unscalable by reason—are all one thing.

It cannot be called "despair" and it is improper to describe it by any such sensational epithet. It may be indicated generally by the term "unknown," but even that is nothing more than a word standing for a negation. Yet, amazing to relate, just there where knowledge is absent, men purport to believe that at that *edge*, at those *bounds*, somewhere below the supernatural, knowledge begins. It is an amazing presumption.

But how say anything of the unknown or qualify it by any means whatever? It is however the basis of all knowledge—rationalizations as evolved in the schools. The only ones who have evoked it solidly are the prerational savages.

Yet there is a palpable mode by which this "beginning" is universally objectified, where it centers not as a mystery, and that is place.

This is the mode by which all the prelogical is made known to us, the unknowable, the "beginnings" of whatever it may be.

Consciousness, which is of all things thinkable the most immaterial, is placed in the breast of man. To think of it as

131

detached, separately operable is impossible. But where else shall one place it?

Precisely that it is unknown but that it is objectified about, is always by place. It is not just to presume analogies that what we do is "like" reality. What we elaborate is worthless, but a kind of wisdom. How then worthless: a presumption that cannot be said—either way. It is merely knowledge. The best we can do with it is rid it of pretense —which has no *place* in it.

Before this knowledge begins it must be placed.

Above everything else if knowledge is to be salvaged at all it must be placed anterior to psychology and leave that strictly alone. It must be located *outside* the mind.

To say the inorganic, the organic and the ethical world are absolutely separate is not true—for an analogy of "truth" runs thru all three. They are like each other in many respects, such as the capability of being divided into primary units which are basic, etc., all three susceptible to approach by any of the methods known to us, the scientific, philosophical or utilitarian.

There is a place, anterior to all philosophical, aesthetic, or scientific arguments actively. It is the basis upon which all rests. It is the same whether that from which—

There is a certain position of the understanding anterior to all systems of thought, as well as of fact and of deed— that is common to all: it is that in which the thinker places himself on the near side of reality—abjures the unknowable and begins *within* a certain tacitly limited field of human possibility to seek wisdom.

This is the field I choose to deal with here. No matter what actively he may go into later—it is outside of my concern—whether he takes that side or this side, practical affairs, philosophy, science, or aesthetics. But the moment he is undecided which, they are beyond, to the right.

This position has its counterpart in all.

It is the past, (from which man has come). It is the "night mind," the chaos, the source of religion; the preconscious, the savage, the animal, the plant, the inorganic—what you will.

But it is none of these. It is one: all tentatives fit into it, not it into them. It is particularly not "the past" out of which knowledge or consciousness going "up" proceeds, leaving it behind. It exists co-incidentally with consciousness, systems, is not escaped.

Objectified, it is place itself—on which all arguments fall.

From this earliest emplacement of thought springs the individual sanction to hold himself superior to all thought without which every practice is baseless. Unless a man be thus placed as all men are in their past—everything subsequent is without foundation.

It is unescapable that on this, emplacement of the understanding, everything else rests, every action, thought, system.

Order is nothing else than one of the kinds of affirmation of the same thing: "place." That is the basis—not order is some charm in itself. It affirms man as the judge of all his own activities. Conscience—dual because impure—that *is* the imperfection of man, the duality of his conscience: pity and ruthlessness, feeling and the lack of it: we seek a place for judgment.

Taking the conscience objectively not as a pawn in the game of philosophy but the practice of human life. Never can it be certain but even the greatest consciences of history shake and vary, fail to agree and commit atrocities offensive to thought as well as to humanity—friend to the perpetuation of disease, the cause of injuries,—and a very bad guide since it inevitably (being a symptom) points with the wind, a vane, an effect of other actions: its basis is to seek a place on which to rest the emotions.

Theory of the convenient, the democrat, the aristocrat—without defense, objectively for the moment America is a democracy—placed there the changes will have a certain contour and action, a corresponding one. Not right, wrong —successful or unsuccessful, but granted a democracy—the U.S.A.—the approach to knowledge, the [initiation] into whatever system of activity may unroll.

Adolescence is this position of an individual gain, this firmness of the individual in adolescence—or see that pre-systematic period as the period of emplacement: so the man who has "worked" or has seen at least from a position of place purely, without other character, enters his education well prepared. He is democratic in that he shares this not by gifts of family like an aristocrat (a great advantage, position—but dangerous to the mind since it involves a confusion, the lesser *seeming* to hold the greater). A commoner might be greater if he feel a community in *this* and so an *addition* to his consciousness and not a division of it among all in common. But a democracy is certainly antagonistic to this realization of place. It hates it, tears down fences that delineate, is jealous of differences,—distrusts all elevations of the realization of intense place, sets a premium on placelessness.

All the avenues to knowledge are alike, all offer the same opportunities, the same rewards, the same deceits. This is no treatise to help choose a profession. It is to place the first steps to the acquisition of knowledge in the United States—and the difficulties involved, what should be avoided, what embraced, and why. For it is more important to know why knowledge is to be held as dear, than to have the knowledge itself. Since everyone has knowledge, all of it is alike—but few know how rightly to value it.

Thus disorder, can at the time when order becomes sterile, placeless, inane—take its place to split the thing it stands for from the "false," "the immoral." Thus alternate the classic and the natural—each to renew the other as place loses significance either way.

Beware of psychologic supports to thought and action—these are a late development not yet certainly placed. First rely on the direct observation of the senses, of such strength everything else is built up, without it nothing is reliable. Judge by the eyes and ears, touch and taste—reject everything from no matter what source that is without a place there.

Conscience the same (as order), it has never been stable —hence the theory of forgiveness. When its order becomes sterile, it must be broken—as with every living thing.

Adolescence is not a unique condition, an undevelopment, negative, the shadow of something else. But positive. It shares with a number of other things its quality of being anterior to systematic knowledge: The past of man, the anomatic, the Socratic acknowledgement of the humanity of knowledge. This quality is that of position, place, and so place is that which most in adolescence is to be appraised and acknowledged.

[Francis Bacon and Shakespeare]

JUNE 28.

The most curious and illuminating compliment that could have been paid to Francis Bacon was for men to have imagined that he wrote the plays of Shakespeare.

And of equal note, especially in relation to the present thesis, is it to realize that in such a fusion, if a confusion of understanding, it is tacitly taken for granted that the knowledge in the essays and the plays being of one time are of one piece. But they are not.

Thus, by luck, the scene is set in an actual and large scale congregate for just the resolutions I propose to display.

This figure may be continued for it is interesting in itself —in addition to creating the note.

Certainly one mind, Bacon's, wished to lay down laws, to settle things about modes. The other spent a life thinking in diversified concretions—and grew more diverse, more removed by "laws," the characters more complex, more "lifelike," the further his thought advanced, and chose finally as his own favorite—a character so split by the impossibility of settled abstraction as to be Hamlet.

No two men working with a common lump of fact could go further in opposite directions than these.

In Shakespeare the characters *are* his thought, the grains of it, and of his life. Bacon "tools all knowledge for his sphere"—which is exactly the same as a man who takes horses or anything for his sphere, provided he go far enough. It is anticlockwise, it is analytic, it is "inhuman."

Whereas thought that is a person, a character, a king— tends to embrace life and become human.

I am presenting just typical instances of—

136

Shakespeare

APRIL 11, 1930.

The impossibility of placing a value other than a humane one on such writings, rare if not unique, as the plays of Shakespeare (and many of the books of the Bible), tends to their apotheosis or rejection by ordered thought. For God is, definitely, the vulgum; scholars, partialists who shed their difficulties to solve some part of them—and so find no relief in that which includes themselves, but only torment.

It is a tremendous cleavage which no one yet has known how to reconcile, this between the surge of the unscholarly gist, the disordered inclusiveness, taking form (or no form) in nature (but with which art must be concerned) and the intellect which bridles—and the careful refinements of the arts.

Yet to grasp the great trouble involved might be the most rewarding imaginable of literary study—and the most humane. It is more avoided than faced. And the slighting of it takes many forms, from the ascribing Shakespeare's plays to Bacon in order to avoid the implicatons of "chance"— in that Shakespeare probably was a fairly ignorant man, through the hair-splitting of schoolroom discipline to the complete—the primitive ignoring of the problems involved— the funny papers.

It is implicit in the one serious trend of thought today— the humanization of knowledge, that is, its adjustment to the facts—the background of all change in schools of thought—

But just as Shakespeare has had no influence on English literature that is not a bad one, so what we do remains a beginning and an end in itself. That is, unless we create a new formal category outside of and opposed to the classical

137

modes which date back step by step to Greece and elsewhere we must remain unclassifiable and "lost."

We must create our basis, that is in criticism as well as works themselves if we are to survive save as provincials in the art. If we will take the situation seriously in hand as a new people we cannot go back to the classic mode but in the manner of Shakespeare (not in the *style* of Shakespeare) follow his naturalism to a neglected conclusion—a wholly new literature.

This is a revolution far beyond the so-called "revolution of the word" than which nothing is more classical.

Has no one seen that all the schools from the beginning, by teaching to write like this, teach men to create not classics but exoticisms, precisely as when, in imitating Negro music, they miss the essence, which is that they must have the form it has because of its naturalism, because it is *Negro* music, and that to do something similar we would have to do something that would be the music of the *whites*. The chief virtue of Negro music apart from its novelty and aphrodisiac character is that it is naturalistic and not by any stretch of the imagination classic.

Thus the real revolution in literature as in all the arts is not formal in the derivative classical sense but a break with all that is taught and an emphasis on all that is *learned*.

There is a unique element in Shakespeare, unique that is, up until his time, that has baffled scholarship which has been at a loss to place it, a new element, a "naturalism" which clashed with all earlier and classic formalizations.

And why not? Shakespeare knew nothing of these things. He wrote outside the scholarly tradition. One must make a choice in accepting his work: either he is a menace to the best in literature or the classic mode has been discovered by him in a fault.

Shakespeare came as an ebullient naturalism of his time. He was thrown out, so to speak, fully grown by his mother (England), a nation breaking through its bounds, whose London was a teapot of languages, whose odors filled the scene. Shakespeare in absorbing all this gratis, almost through his skin, was braced, intoxicated, fed and released all in one.

He, Shakespeare, occupied in relation to his world the precise position America, as a nation, occupies toward the classical culture of Europe or the East today. We at our best (so far) are not scholars but we have wit, alert sensibilities. Our problem before the world is precisely his: shall we be accepted because of our species of "naturalism" or rejected because we do not meet the qualifications of scholarship?

The parallelism is complete save only that we have not produced work comparable to his. But that should be the criterion. It is in the force of our direct "naturalistic" observation that we shall succeed and not by tagging behind those who, in a different understanding, we cannot approach —but must admire.

This is the place occupied by America.

What should be taught in colleges, what else can be taught than the usual curriculum? The answer is not to change the curriculum but for the men to change their attitude toward what is taught. In fact it is changed now and will change more but the change has not been sufficiently recognized. It is, briefly, the reiteration of the man himself who finds himself not below the classics but comparable to them. Level, free to understand, which he is never when he is put to school to "learn" them.

This is truly the "cultural" aspect of a general education so-called but it has not been isolated, clarified. What *is* this cultural aspect that comes creeping in with classified study (perhaps): It is not scholarship, not degrees, not snobbism of knowledge, not knowledge of the classics at all but a liberation of the man himself. He might, possibly, feel himself like the thought which he absorbs from his reading just as another man might gain the same by other means.

A liberal education needs the dignity of a new recognition. It will have to take into consideration a naturalism, typified by the works of Shakespeare, unplaced in, if not antagonistic to, the usual "classical" approach, and in this the "new world" has its opportunity, and not in going back on its tracks in the old way—tho' to no other end.

The approach to learning through the classics, called, let us say, the classical approach, can be lethal to the intelligence. As young men we feel it, the antagonism to "Latin" is not pure laziness. The schools have taken their toll, without question. Unless the knowledge offered is first placed, understood to be what it is, an accessory to the fact, it is dangerous. This is seldom if ever understood in the schools.

It can be easily conceived that with a classical training, Shakespeare would have been thoroughly gelded. He might easily have fallen into definition, whereas his chief fecundity derives from just the escape his lack of schooling offered. He saw at first hand with the dignity of a discoverer. It is he who breaks the school to escape who has the best chance of survival.

The whole scheme needs revision.

McAlmon survives. Eliot fails.

The Logic of Modern Letters, Primary

THIS SUGGESTS certain conclusions, relative to an education based upon this peculiar American inopportunity, occasion and lack—absolute and perfect—shows up futile objective—tedious deserts of information—fossil tracks—falsely directed profundities.

Language is made up of words and their configurations, (the clause, the sentence, the poetic line—as well as the subtler, style); to these might be added the spaces between the words (for measurement's sake) were these not properly to be considered themselves words—of a sort.

Language is again divided according to its use into two main phases. 1. That by which it is made secondary to the burden of ideas—information, what not—for service to philosophy, science, journalism. This includes the gross use of language. And 2. where language is itself primary and ideas subservient to language. This is the field of letters, whence the prevalence of fiction and the preeminence of poetry in this division.

These two major uses of language complement each other—or should in a well-adjusted intelligence.

In the modern American world the proper interrelationship between the two is hardly understood at all. The practice of letters is neglected with serious results—sensed but dumbly even by the ablest.

A scrutiny of the common use of language for the use of ideas—the idea-mongering (keeping the divisions in mind) makes it obvious and simple that such use is an anomaly. That both science and philosophy even, are making use of something properly outside their sphere.

Language under such circumstances is really debauched—prostituted in the sense that it is enforced for a purpose by which it is limited strictly to nonlinguistic necessities.

By this it is tied to ideas by word and configuration with useful results but with fatal effect due to the character of language itself.

It goes down through as the activities by which words are raped for the pleasure or necessity of another purpose, religious, scholarly, construction or whatever it may be. Down to legal use or, worse still, the use of language among legislative bodies where its degradation is complete.

Here it is used as a means for the imposition of manners, customs, by cupidity, ineptitude, or quite as importantly by the able imposers of political ideas.

For of course it must be seen that legislation is the use of language for the stabilization and availability of political ideas. This is of course proper.

Language is subordinated by this and by language that takes these configurations of laws, statutes, we ourselves (along with the words) are deeply enslaved. It is language reduced to its lowest state.

But even when it is most successful, in the constitution of a country, in the Constitution of the United States, it is still language subservient to ideas.

Note two parallel statements, one by Jefferson, one by Ibsen, etc. etc.

It is by language that we are stabilized and by changing, the sense drops out of the language. So that in the end the debauchery becomes complete—without continued inventions.

Letters, in which language is primary and ideas subservient to it—is the salutary loosing of words and their configurations from stultifying combinations with their users.

Language. (trace down thru modern poetry).

Poetry, unchartered, is mediaevalism capitalized.

Reality of the word.

Children—approximate the result that would be obtained. Then take up bit about school.

Summary: The Logic of Modern Letters
(Last Chapter)

(a *few* written words because I
wish to phrase them carefully)

POETRY IS MADE of (just) words, like the anatomy books,
the books of philosophy—only it is words used with a
broader sweep of understanding, a better knowledge of
their capabilities, a greater accuracy—words raised to [their]
highest power. But the baser use predominates and has had
serious repercussions in thought, and so manners, customs—
uncontrollable by science or philosophy. Nothing but poetry
can readjust the understanding (sold to books) to a reason-
able view of the world.

This is at the base of modern letters—of modernism—its
inevitability—its inescapable logic. As an occupation of the
intelligence it surpasses all other functions of the mind in
practical interest and serviceability. Incredible. It is, being at
the base of knowledge itself, neglected. Perverted. Avoided.
Misunderstood.

It is to divorce words from the enslavement of the prev-
alent clichés that all the violent torsions (Stein, Joyce)
have occurred; violent in direct relation to the gravity and
success of their enslavements.

Language, bearing this relation to the understanding, is
the care of men of letters. Take the Constitution of the U. S.
We were fortunate in having Jefferson to phrase it—a major
part of its durability, no doubt. Tho' he joins Ibsen in a
curious observation men of letters are alert to (with genius):
Jefferson said that liberalism is not assured without a revolu-
tion every 20 years. And Ibsen said that a truth becomes a
lie in 20 years. Why? Language is the answer. It is because
men grow away from the quality of language which insured
them stability and which so goes dead.

143

Does it not occur to someone to stress the reality of the word—as distinguished from the things which the word engages and which kill it finally?

This calls for creative writing—that is what it means: a contemporary use of words and conformations of words— dropping from them the overburdening clichés of science, history, philosophy and imbecility—not slang, not the journalese—but poetry—a difficult thing, not above all in America—"English."

Some avoid this apparent necessity—this self-apparent— and do charming things—even defend their position ably—.

The work of T. S. Eliot has had a notable vogue.

(read Eliot, Pound—etc., H. D., Stein and Joyce—E. E. Cummings—etc., McAlmon.

NOT include myself here. Just read a few of my things from the early type to the most modern—showing language changes etc.)

This is what goes with it—.

This is the care over the placing of a dot, a capital. This agony of mind shared by all—a helplessness.—That one does by action—a poet does by his style.

It is his affair to find a way out and for the spirit, heart, soul—one for all together, a net to hold the whole intelligence and life of a man: peculiarly a poet's.

The Logic of Modern Poetry

WE EAT, married comfort in bed, adulteries—as if we were
alone to enjoy, (how can we share it—no one knows)—
—a catalogue–
We see the stupidity of love—
A man's own little shrinking personality: Byron.
We have only poetry to offer—not a sloppy appeal—
A style to offer—(not our business to say whether or not
it is of value) it is what we have—

—and for this we are given the archaic oxcart and—modes
of a past—whole matter is dead to us—
Sonnet, rhymes, capital letter and we are told that this is
important.
Some measure yes, but a new one.
Why?

Before education (which is in itself the preliminary view)
we require a view of knowledge which is at the same time
comprehensive, obvious and simple. Something an infant
might grasp, a thing now lacking.
Letters gives us precisely the detachment for this view. It
gives us the vantage of a view over knowledge by which
to evaluate it in its totality. Placed, it can be approached.
Joe Cook's mechanisms are a splendid satire.

(A Sketch for) The Beginnings of an American Education

1. BOY'S ACTUAL EXPERIENCE.

2. From this vantage, this detachment from the informative preoccupations of modern periods of the intelligence —an American break (typified in the presumed break America was supposed to make in the European bulwark) almost obliterated—

3. Schools, colleges—the arrangement of the *places* to be occupied by knowledge—subservient to the intelligence— that has stepped out of bounds—

4. French painting (example).

5. Shakespeare—the pure "language man"—offered as a critical comprehension—as the *effect* of the stand taken—

6. The Logic of Modern Letters.

Shakespeare is a man almost pure—of language, offers the example of what the change in attitude toward learning —unique in him will (or may) accomplish. Socrates the other—

Where an education is at fault, basically, the correction of it had better begin in the schools where the fault is probably entrenched—under the name of some banner of authority—

A good beginning in this case would be to abolish in American schools (at least) all English departments and to establish in [their] place the department of Language—of which the English could be a subsidiary—one of the divisions—or not, as it may be desired.

It is not a language that is desired—but language; for in that and its phases and functions a great—lies for correcting gross faults of perspective in the whole structure of the modern intelligence—the department of letters: where all scholarship begins: it is so obvious and simple that the significance seems trite—

The use of language by science and philosophy is an expedient because of which strong limitations are put upon its range of effectiveness. It must never, as a means, either in science or philosophy or the other correlated modes (such as history, religion, and the legislative uses—also journalism and common speech) transcend the idea which it is put forward to represent.

It is in these modes a symbol without reality of its own. Thus it has no reality apart from the thing, movement, event, which it is put to represent.

But in letters the complement of this use of language exists. Words and their configurations become preeminent and (precisely as the manner indicated above) ideas, movements, facts, are the symbols which it uses (or escapes them when it will).

In this case words and their configurations are the reality and the full use of language realized. The only use that can be scientifically and philosophically sanctioned, is that of letters.

"It has always been so in history, that an entire generation has owed its outward freedom to the inner freedom of one individual."

My country, right or wrong.

"The book as a whole is a whole."

TO
MY BOYS—
Wishing them luck—

[The Pluralism of Experience]

EVERYTHING RESTS, so far as I can see, on a condition, obvious to the eye, which may be called, if one care to, the pluralism of experience. And, obviously, no "law" or abstract summary can include this since in itself it stands outside a generalization, it is plural concretely and in fact.

This has not been sufficiently realized in thought: it is crudely stated in the multiples of Pagan mythology, in the politics of "Democracy" and in such inborn feelings as nationalism, "states' rights," etc. etc.

Its present use to me—

It offers this release—life, continued productivity not only in fish eggs but thought.

It is opposed by the pinching academy which tries to relegate it to paleontology, to the "crude beginnings," to an earlier condition. But it is as new—so new, that it will shortly be the newest, most pregnant motivation of thought and life in the world.

It is decentralizing in effect as opposed to the merely opportunistic tendencies (due to the surrounding barbarism of the world) of centralization—in the sciences, arts, etc.

Quickly, it is this: that every individual, every place, every opportunity of thought is both favored and limited by its emplacement in time and place. Chinese 8th cent., Italian 12th, English 15th, French 18th, African, etc. All sorts of complicated conditions and circumstances of land, climate, blood, surround every deed that is done.

Due to certain conditions there flourishes a "school" of thought, Western, Eastern. It is one. It brings to a certain perfection that which it can do—and then can do no more—without destruction first. It has flowered.

149

Now, America is such a place. The old cultures *cannot*, can never without our history, our blood or climate, our time of flowering in history—can never be the same as we. They cannot.

We all work side by side for the same things (tho' we don't know what these things are) but the impasses of older cultures are not ours. And these impasses are intrinsic in their work, their beginnings enforce them, to destroy their history would be just to destroy themselves. We may and surely will find impasses but they will be different from theirs.

Thus we are to work in our own "locality": not piggishly, not narrowly. We must see, steal, beg, borrow—but we borrow only that *which we want*. What we feel, think, conclude that we need. Not what is imposed on us (unless we can't help it, then we use that too: Negro American music).

And the justice of this is that by such pluralism of effort in each several locality a "reality" is kept; in plural—and so verified.

By success in many places on different planes our efforts are confirmed, not driven to defeat and pessimism as in the case of mere central supremacy—which is in effect a denial of reality, not its consummation. Each school enhances the perfection of some other. But all strongly sanction—all. And enrich. But a later "school" must have as great leeway—and it will—it is insured to thought in the limitations of each "perfection."

Five Philosophical Essays

Foreword

THESE FIVE ESSAYS may represent a struggle, or a phase of one in which every man becomes involved: to be at peace in his own mind. To resolve my own difficulties I have herein attempted to systematize my thoughts: to concentrate them: to separate them into units and to look at them. That I have not completely succeeded is of course entirely to be understood yet in that I have been able to make several solid steps toward my object these notes deserve to be kept as records and will be kept as such.

1. Faith and Knowledge

UPON A GREAT round hot and cold mass of eighty odd indestructible materials I am thrust in an unconscious state. Here I am whirled about through an unfathomable space while other great round masses, some all ablaze, whirl past by me at great distances. Later I become conscious and find about: creatures like myself and a great number of other objects alive, all made of the same materials as the mass; principally of four, three of which are gases, airs.

These things alive move, grow, change, are of many colors and shapes and become familiar. Then they lose their color, cease to move, become dry, break up and return to the hot and cold mass; the more or less separate indestructible materials again.

Questioning why they did not stay with me I am told that they are dead and that their life is ended; that all life ends so, as mine will also and that this is a law of nature. For a day I miss them and look in dark corners and push the ashes with a stick but they are really gone. Whither? Yet it sticks in my mind that this is a natural law.

Meanwhile I may sit in the sun and sing because my father and mother bring me food. About is sunshine and moonshine; trees that are green and cool and full of birds that I hear singing. I am happy. Then grubs consume the flowers, storms, lightning and pests kill the trees, the birds freeze in the snow, I myself with my house under a cliff returning see it crushed flat by an immense stone. I begin to fear; I am unhappy. "Is this law?" I may well cry. Against law I am set then. I feel it pursue me, feel in it an evil and a tyranny. In winter I can freeze. The snow and ice creep at me. In summer the streams are all treacherous currents. Time itself and distance crush me on all sides like enemies, for to the south is food. Well; but it is afar therefore of no use to me. Thus space can tyrannize. In the spring was food, in the spring will be food; Yes, but what of now? Thus time crushes me. I am a slave then to this law which is ever at my throat; I fear it and make of other creatures and things sacrifices that its anger may be thus sated before it reaches to me. Oh but if it be waiting for me to rend me after I die! The thought is too horrible to bear and I rush off to forget by any means, best by some madness of excess. Later I awake to cry that I did not come into the world of my own accord and to curse my parents and all things and wish I had never been and that I were dead—but I am afraid to die.

Being alone I by this time begin to starve. I must work to live and being afraid to perish I straightway begin by planning to enjoy to the full my senses and for the rest —it is law.

Work then begins. At once I find that by mounting a horse I am freed against much of the tyranny of distance; that by placing boards so, I can store grain against the tyranny of time, I find that frost loosens rocks. They fall and crush houses and so I no longer live under a cliff but in the open and thus begin to be freed from the tyranny of chance. I look about and see the drought come and the flowers fade, but I have water stored in a rock; the storms come and the trees are ripped apart but I know where to hide; snow comes and the birds freeze but I have my fire. I am better off than they. How? By these same tyrant laws, because I know them and predict and provide against. "Oh great Knowledge," I say, "thou hast taken my part against this bloody brutal law."

On and on through the generations and law is the same but I have changed. I have found that against the tyranny of the law I have a power, knowledge, to make me no longer its slave but its master, that law serves me and not I it. I am grown in strength then by these laws which have become my servants through knowledge. Yet the fear, the belief that knowledge is merely standing between me and desolation still remains.

Suddenly, as is quite usual in such cases I have found, a new strength springs up: "If you have been able to provide against one law by knowledge and also against many laws you will be able to provide against all even against that last one which is death, for there is no tyranny but ignorance." It is faith sprung out of experience! Faith which inquiry not destroys but deepens. My very heart bounds! I am free! Away! Let me have knowledge, all of it, always more and more. But first I pause as on a high hill and look about.

Behind is knowledge like a great plain with green and yellow plants and bare places whereabout I have walked marking with my hands so that a misty system of leading paths now stretches through all in an incomplete but regular way. But as I turn about yonder stretches the unknown!

Let me bow my head in labor then, but before I go I will build here a monument to this new thing, faith, and dedicate it to the mystery before me that I may look up from my labor when I am weary and remember how I am thinking now and here. And I will bring the fruits of my labors to be a symbol and a sign that I am working and have accomplished; that I know a little but the mystery is before me wherein through knowledge I will find freedom. Now I descend to my plain to work and I find others and we are all together. And we are happy for now nothing seems to be able to make us unhappy since faith has sprung out of knowledge, banishing fear to make us so.

But now come men in stuffs made of dead animals, plants and minerals dextrously prepared and fitted to hang over their shoulders and fit over their feet to protect them, and keep them soft, and shine in the sun, all of which I have made. They put a twig with green leaves on my head and say this: "Poor man, at last you have found faith, but here it was from the first if you would have taken it. Yet knowledge has done well and so we crown it, but your search is futile, abandon it; abandon your bare altar and come with us for the end of knowledge is but to find faith. Cease to labor for with faith the rest will come to pass without your seeking. Have you no faith in heaven? But only in yourself, you puny man?" Yet are they cloaked out in my symbols which I have made.

Where is my content now? Yet I must answer them or they will overbear me and so I begin: "You would have me be as this little child here, would you?" "Yes," they say. "Just as you find him." Then I say, "Yet leave these children without my knowledge which I have given to their parents and many of them will suffer horribly and die because of bad milk; I have seen them. Who are you better than I unless you have more knowledge than I? My word for yours; here is my answer. When you strip from you the garments I have made and when you have destroyed your convenient devices and your things of beauty such as I have discovered and made for symbols and that you may live safely and conveniently according to law; when you live without the effects of knowledge then come to me and I will listen. Go build for yourselves a village in some desolate place without knowledge and see how you fare. Do these things and convince me. When you have done them I will believe you have discovered more than I know and I will follow but now I have a master who has served me well in return for my services and as I am a man I believe I shall follow knowledge as long as I exist for by knowledge alone have I come upon faith and in no other way. Then unless he have knowledge, let no man say of this mystery anything but that it is a mystery, but if you will predict into the mystery by faith, you must do it by knowledge; in no other way.

"Or at any rate this is my way which is not forbidden by better knowledge or in any other way. It is mine and you shall not deprive me of it, for this cannot be gainsaid: he who will not be a slave to natural law, which is all the law we know, must conquer it. To conquer it there is no way but by knowledge. I hold in my own choice my fate to be a slave, only myself being able to free myself and that only through knowledge. I do not despise you, I do not even know what you are or what I am; I will not take anything from you nor do I seek to make you as I am, but I will neither yield to you what I have in order to believe unless I receive in return all I have ever had and more which you do not offer. With me it is only by what I know that I can indicate further what I do not know and so be led to believe."

2. Beauty and Truth

FILLED WITH the desire of a child to look about, to explore, I find myself frequently in company with one of my own age. Each being provided for as to food and other living necessities, we give our senses considerable play, choosing fields and woods to roam. At times we come upon men speaking quietly from books and, being inexperienced, we listen intently and are able to catch much that is said. One speaks: "Remember, whatever the aspect of any activity, any change, may be, whether organic or inorganic, psychic or chemical, it is but an expression in the one material which is itself not changed; that by these expressions only can we know anything and that by what we know only can we indicate further what we do not know and so believe." Another speaks: "It has not been conceived that two stones and two stones can, taken together, become either more or less than four stones and so with all other objects whatever, never two and two will make but four and never four but resolved will disclose two and two. So we say in terms which themselves have no meaning but represent and stand for merely, in terms we say, a whole is the sum of its parts, a law of mathematics. Further, it is not conceived of a time in the past when this law did not hold nor of a time in the future when it will not hold permanent. Nothing else is conceivable. So it is with all laws whatever, once seen nothing else is conceivable and we speak of these laws as permanent by which we prophesy, show faith, that they will endure. Man has never invented a law but his most complex devices and mechanisms were, with knowledge and application, as possible in Egypt and before, as now. Man, then, but discovers, and neither creates nor can he either destroy except images, expressions. Then if all has been and will be, beyond conception to the contrary, all truth is now and here, in part discovered and, manifestly, in part only expressed." Stirred though bewildered by these speeches, we set forth anew, our aimless instinct yet gaining head and promising to gain, perhaps, even a direction. "Let us find truth!" we cry with others, but to express it? Fie! will it not express itself? Perhaps. In that we two are of so identical a taste we therefore continue together with an ever increasing interest in all things.

By this time we have begun to record our impressions and after several years of mutually enjoyed association we disclose our brief jots each to the other. Here is a remarkable difference where we had reasonably, we thought, supposed none to be, thinking instead to find a remarkable similarity if not an identity in the matter, for we were attracted to the same things, at the same time, observed them together with an equal interest. Looking at our papers laid side by side, true, our notes are similar in this, that they are of colors, shapes, shades, sounds, scent and motion but there the similarity ends. Mine are all of form itself and motion: a sweet berry relished, a bird's flight enjoyed. But his are of the structure of form and the function of motion: how a berry plant draws sugar from dirt, how a bird offsets gravity.

At once a discussion arises in which, surprised anew, we discover the strength of our hidden difference. For, though we had imagined we were seeking one and together, my companion still passionately declares for truth and champions analysis to find it while I, with equal passion, declare for truth but pretend to find it in beauty. Desirous of continuing together as we are going, each strives to convince the other of his error but failing, we decide with reluctance that we must part. We are sorry for this but occasion leading us different ways, we go gladly.

I set out at once, "If beauty is here I will find it for I

love it more than life." By which I tacitly assert my belief that I will know beauty when I see it, though in truth I have not the slightest idea what it will look like as if it would look like anything other than itself. Yet surely it will be nature; all that is beautiful should, taken together, be all beauty, I think. Thus, unconsciously I have already placed all beauty in a coat of dirt since all expressions of activity and form are in the same material—unless perhaps all beauty is not expressed. But this does not occur to me.

I turn then to nature to find beauty. I will seek it in clouds, in trees, in man, in beasts, in all that is: well—except I leave out the one individual of the most marvelous creation of nature of which I know most; myself. Or rather I cannot leave him out but I strive to forget him as stubbornly as possible.

In a short time, however, I begin to realize that I am not seeing the thing, beauty, but trees over and over and over. I get nowhere, I am standing still!

Now however, in the midst of my sublime search, this self, this me, begins to assert itself, to be manifest and interrupts my doubts with gnawings in what I call the heart. I begin to crave to express this nature that I see, though why express is not plain, for if beauty is here, all I have to do is to find it. Why express? This is pure vanity. Right. I will not, I will go on with my work—yet shortly I am beginning to try my hand at the moulding of form in various materials often cursing the desire to "push—a dripping point." Yet I must.

Words do not satisfy me; I will take colors and go out. Now I understand! I will go out; I will not only see this beauty, find it, but I will make it mine. Mine, mine, as if I can possess anything. Further than that, I will give, I will give the beauty to the world in my expression. What, is nature so poor that her work must be done a second time, or have you ceased to search entirely and now are merely exhibiting? To give to the world in my expression! The thought comes with a thrill of delight. Now I think I know why I am being urged to express. It is that beauty may be given larger scope. Yes, I have ceased to search, it is true, I have gone into exhibitions.

I go forth gladly, then, looking at the sky, the streams, the trees, with a big heart to make this beauty mine.

The progress now takes on a color of exhilaration. I find that there will be joy in doing, in the very act. Here then I will sit in my sublime but brittle mood and work. Result, blots, smudges, lies, I cannot do it! I am frantic with impatient desire. Flinging down colors I spring to words, worse; to clay, I can do nothing. Of music I know nothing. Wheeling about, distracted, at each opening a door is slammed in my face and I become a prisoner in myself for I cannot express anything much less the beauty in nature.

From no virtue of my own but in my own spite and by the grace of a few million years of more or less hardy ancestors I stumble back to colors in a vain pet not to be beaten, unconsciously beginning to work and at last forgetting all about my sublime search and in fact of beauty altogether. Thus the search being forgotten I am at last truly started in the trail of beauty. Or else at times I remember the search and at once fall to cursing this ugly mass of material that has spoilt my simple delight, floating down upon me like a cloud in which I am struggling merely. However for the most part I am too much engrossed in work to think of anything else than its details in arrangement and expedience.

The result is surprising to a novice: I at once begin to see that I am moving somewhere, for objects I have passed begin to lie behind me. Perhaps I am moving even toward beauty? But at least by my work I am moving. Then at last it dawns on me: "I myself am moving myself! Oh wonderful!"

Again I go forth to nature for now I can express.—What is that? I have looked at that tree a thousand times but— Lord! I can see! I have learnt to see! by my work I have learnt to see!

I go back to my labor almost wild with joy for now, now I will learn to see beauty and when I go forth again it will be to make one grand final expression! All the scattered parts of beauty shall be collected into one perfect whole! (For men to stare at as if it were a stuffed bird, I might have added.)

At least I am learning to express, to put what I see into symbols and finally, after unending experiments aided by some natural aptitude I feel ready to go forth, to perform my masterpiece, not thinking of the emptiness of the world after I had corralled all of beauty and not thinking of my own few lonely days to live after the great achievement. "I will sum every mood of existing things," and do not doubt but that I am competent, for at the end of my probation, believe me when I say, there is none that I cannot excell in the accuracy of eye to distinguish the finest variations of form shade and color or in the dexterity of hand to express all that is seen.

I go forth! I even succeed! It is the marvel of all eyes! All eyes but mine. The world gapes at it in amazement but I—where is my joy? Where is beauty? Fled like the proverbial bird from its cage. I am crushed with disappointment.

Then beauty is not in nature. For surely it is not the material of which nature is made yet all that nature expresses is expressed here in my masterpiece. Yet I am not fool enough to fail to see that the thing I have done is beautiful, as beautiful as nature but it just as surely is not all beauty. Why then nature is not all beauty; the conclusion is inevitable. It has taken me long enough to learn this.

I sit down or walk up and down and think. This is a new sensation, this thinking, but I pursue it with my usual energy. Nature is not beauty, then, but it is beautiful. Then it expresses beauty: beauty is in nature; it is in a tree but it is not a tree. What is this beauty then but a ghost? The idea seems preposterous, funny even. Beauty has no form but it is expressed in form; it is in nature but all of it is not in nature for then I would have found it. It is then, in indefinite part, unexpressed all about me awaiting expression. But how am I to find it? Oh how unless you feel it in your own heart, you fool.

The thought is excellent. Surely man is the most marvelous in our nature. Here then, perhaps, will most beauty find expression. Why it is here in me fairly aching to be freed in the semblance of a leaf or anything. In me is beauty such as nature elsewhere never dreamt of, here in myself waiting for expression. I no longer see trees but beauty in form of trees and thus a new life. All nature now becomes a symbol for me to use. This I have earned and now, now comes a joyous moment when I begin to win beauty from the air, to give it life, Heaven knows what, to bring it out of torment, perhaps; to clasp that which never was in heaven nor on earth, to create and bid the very essence live with me.

To search, to discover, to win more and more to myself, to pursue ever and express is now become all life to me. I can see no other life.

By this time I have arrived at some degree of eminence among men, when, glancing up one day, I am not a little pleased, perhaps even a little surprised to find my old friend the scientist quite as eminent as I. He regards me confidently a while but occasion throwing us now together as it had thrust us apart, we inquire each of the other, his experiences. I having finished, my friend begins:

At the outset, much as you did, I sought—I will be very brief—to find all truth. I would investigate all things and when all things were investigated I would have the perfection. This was exceedingly simple, the only other necessity being energy.

Forthwith I examined and analyzed everything I could lay hand upon until I had examined everything. This naturally took some time, say three million years. At the end it was plain that there are but a few very simple and permanent materials out of which all other things are made. Here, then, was truth and the end of knowledge, yet I was not satisfied. I would look further, but since all that it was possible for me to see lay before me my desire to see more obviously had its difficulties unless the something I sought could not be seen—but this appeared to me as impractical.

I sat down in front of my elements, then, and looked at them rather blankly, I imagine until, to my surprise, they suddenly appeared to my imagination as arrangements of some one ground fiber which became known as electron. Thus, I say my imagination saw them but to my eyes became apparent another arrangement which was very tangible, for these few and so far indestructible elements began to take on a kind of rhythmic order according to weight and density which ascended in a broken scale through them all. A form began to emerge, a law as permanent as the elements themselves, a truth perhaps! Why, I had made a discovery! Here was something not an element yet as permanent as any element.

Interest seized me and in turn I finally grasped the simple fact that all nature is but a complex arrangement; that the few elements, perhaps one, governed by law, take on shapes, form, which cannot be directly analyzed, for as forms they have no substance. At the first attempt your form goes and your elements return. Form can only be discovered and appreciated, not analyzed.

I must confess, this touched my fancy. All nature began to arrange itself as the elements had done, into a remarkable system in which I could detect trends, leadings, and so I discovered other laws, which laws never changed but always shuffled the elements about in an identical way.

Here was something then, this law, which I had never seen, that I could not touch or grasp yet which I knew to exist. I called it an abstraction, then a truth, because it was permanent.

At any rate here was something more than the materials, here was an opening, here then I would seek for truth, for it seemed but a simple step to imagine these laws to be parts of the truth and truth itself—my goal—to be one perfect abstraction that would contain all else, to which you would have added, that since all truth is but expressed in form, perfect truth would be expressed in perfect form, which is beauty.

However true or false this may be I appreciated at once that I could never see these laws directly but only the expression, yet the belief persisted that when all these laws were found expressed, that then I would find all truth. Thus I set forth.

I do not go about it as you do, seeking the perfect form direct, which may be an impossible thing, but instead I strive to find the several laws one by one. Of course I took it for granted that since all law must be conceived as infinitely existing in the past and future, that they exist in the present, that all laws are expressed in nature and that I only need to see the expression to appreciate the law. Your idea of expressing laws that have yet no form not occurring to me, and I am forced to say that the notion seems an extremely one.

The rest is plain: according to this system, which I have outlined to you, I have shaped my endeavor with ever widening fields for research and since I enjoy the exhilaration of work I have not been oppressed by the apparent endlessness of my task. The rest is more detail *ad infinitum*, and quite technical.

However your point of view interests me greatly. We will grant arbitrarily that you are right in saying that all laws are not expressed, with a view to finding where this hypothesis leads us. To begin let me summarize our experiences. We can say as follows:

That as far as we know all that exists now has always existed and will always exist.

That there are a few materials in nature that undergo changes but are themselves unchanged.

That these changes present themselves in arrangements or forms and occur regularly and always the same. We say these changes express laws.

That these laws are not of any material nor do they exist in the material but are expressed by it.

That only by the expression of a law can we know a law; we cannot know a law itself but we can only know a transcription, as it were, of something which we take to be real.

That men cannot think of laws directly but only in terms.

Therefore that though perfect law exist all about him man cannot know it but can only know that part of it which he has found terms for.

That these terms may be any phenomenon or combination of such in nature discovered by analysis or otherwise.

Now then, sir, enters your part of the story:

But further, that man can feel abstractions not existing expressed in man or nature elsewhere, therefore not discoverable by analysis, and can learn to know these abstractions and fit terms to them.

That man can only do this by labor with materials.

That certain laws discovered by analysis, arranging themselves in more gross forms are called "truths," and can be expressed in words and other trite terms but that the more impalpable laws felt are called "beauty," and cannot be expressed in words as terms but must be symbolized with direct figures.

That truth can only be expressed in form: that all truth can only be expressed in perfect form which is all beauty and perfection.

That through the discovery of a more and more nearly completely expressive form, which is beauty in the same terms, it is possible for man to approach nearer and nearer to perfection.

Well perhaps. But let us look about again. We have gotten ourselves well into abstraction, well off the earth and nothing remains but the earth itself, these same troublesome materials which we have neglected. Does it not appear to you as an artist that these abstractions we speak of do not contain these trees and minerals but merely arrange them; that your beauty does not contain your colors but is a very fine law that arranges them? Well, this is no affair of art's, it is for science, but I will say that the very existence of this material is law also, the greatest one of all and that here is the endless mystery of life. It is the fashion of the age to be abstract but the reality of what we see puts a vigor, a sturdiness into one, that is essential. There is but one thing we can know directly and that is the world we own and we do own it, which is not so insignificant a matter after all, even if we must share our star with a few others. And if all truth contains everything, why, is not this world a part of the whole truth, the very existence, a greater mystery than any other mere abstract law? To go about preoccupied is the greatest folly, for if we were suddenly given our abstraction and suspended in ether with both feet off the ground, as we always are in preoccupation, how would we fare, being deprived of the most fascinating part of truth, which forever in sight, we would eternally pine after as now we pine after our abstraction.

Sir, we live in mystery and I can only look with surprise on those who smile pityingly on children and bewail their own lost innocence. What great thing have we found that makes us so much more than children are. The innocence of a child is good but innocence is secure and the innocence of a man is far nobler. Who is not innocent in the face of the mystery? Even ignorance is transformed into beauty by faith.

I hope you are not annoyed to hear me talk this way, I've gotten myself into quite a mood.

Now I have finished. Is it not remarkable to note how nearly you and I, in common with most men, come to agreeing on most subjects and with undoubted forbearance, too?

To watch with clear eyes and to accept truth at any moment from any corner and in most various shapes, to be ready to follow or to lead fearlessly, quite impromptu, is a "parlous" task these days and makes one irritable and slow to relinquish old worn-out customs, especially at our age, eh?

3. Constancy and Freedom

FEW THINGS, when discovered, have been recognized with greater gladness by man than persistency, solidity, permanency, that which through change stays unchanged. In so great a love for this thing, then, according to man's habit we would expect to find it familiarly applied, brought near, made part of the life of this man. And in so far as it is great so do we expect to find it playing a great part. We do find this so. Between individuals it is constancy, which would be the first property of friendship and so true is this that in such intense friendship as is called love, we do not conceive it except as "true" or constant. In affairs it is fidelity, trustworthiness, accountability, reliability; between countries it is national honesty; while all those manifestations which have seemed to man as all persistent he names natural laws, then classifies and divides these laws into his sciences and recognizes them as the property of his highest conception, his divinity, so deeply is this constancy in his respect.

In fact we will say that nothing has been more sought after than this immaterial property, immaterial since we can neither hear, see, nor touch it. Nothing has been sought after with greater zest than this stability unless perhaps it is its opposite, liberty. We say opposite as black is to white, as yes is to no, as motion is to no motion. Liberty shall be the motion and constancy the no motion. Thus we say it seems.

But this liberty, then, has it been so much desired? A thousand examples would appear: the child would be free from the father, the slave from prison, the puritan to think, the free lover from the puritan, the people from oppression.

170

But shall we not find this freedom appearing under other names? familiarized, made the daily companion of man? Yes, also; we call for independence of character, generosity which will let me be different from another or shall we see liberty only in the hatred for tyranny. But in open nature we find other examples; it is universal change, it is the new, it is that no two trees are alike, it is the thrill of surprise, mystery, the unaccountable against the accountable. All this has for a basis, liberty. It is change, then, against the unchanged; the new against the old and permanent. Here, then, is a great controversy, the "I will go," against the "I must stay!"

How better typified than in the great striving everywhere between liberal and conservative, between the steadfastness of age and volatility of youth. It is an ever-present controversy, both sides often abusing one the other. But deeper! Let us look into ourselves. I will be true to you and remain (Says Shelley to his first wife) yet I have occasion to go. I will be a painter but I am a poet; I will know everything but I can know only this thing. This is a far-reaching controversy. Let us look well then that if there really be such a controversy, as it seems, we can take sides and fight more clearly, but if there be none, that fighting be done away with entirely.

Let us examine the two sides, then, to find out the character of each. For if I were to choose between two nuts I would open them first, the better to know how to proceed to determine which were best for eating and which for throwing away.

Liberty or freedom, first, to reverse the order. Here is a man surrounded by blocks of stone so ingeniously piled that he cannot get beyond them on any side, yet he can see between and he sees yonder a green meadow where he would walk except that he cannot get beyond the stones. We say this man is not free for he will walk about in the meadow and cannot.

Release him then. He is in the meadow walking about but

now he would fly in the air but the law of gravity so ingeniously surrounds him that he cannot. Thus, again, he is not free. And thus we find the first property of freedom which we are trying to define: that it can be comparative for there is no other essential difference in these two cases except that of degree. To walk or to fly are of the same nature, simple, nearly related physical acts.

There is no difference then except that here he is tyrannized over by human law and there by natural laws. The only advantage he has gained is in the degree of his freedom: a bigger, roomier for a smaller, more cramped tyranny. No! for see. I will walk, I know well how to walk yet, though I know, I cannot. I would do that which I know how to do yet I cannot. This is human tyranny.

But I would fly yet I do not know how. How now? My ignorance, not law, is the tyrant for now that I know how to fly there is no law to prevent me from doing so. (This "doing" is good.) Then knowledge is ultimate freedom, and knowledge seeks law, natural law, such as we nickname truth or in other terms, permanence or constancy. Thus we have the spectacle of freedom yearning after constancy or permanence in order to be freer.

Knowledge we say is freedom, and our definition of freedom might be knowledge but neither of these statements is true, for we cannot fly by knowledge, we must add action to our knowledge, we must do.

Our freedom then is to live under all the truth, all of it which we know and, as by thought and action new truth is found, if we would be free we must live under that also. But continue the progression until, should all truth be found, which would be absolute permanence since nothing else would remain to cause variation, why then we would have absolute freedom, since freedom can be comparative and is greater, the broader the truth it lives under.

Thus we have absolute freedom and absolute permanence coinciding and perfectly essential one to the other.

It is evident, then, that neither freedom nor constancy is

less important or "true" one than the other and in the sense that one is wrong and the other right there is no remotest controversy between them.

However there is a controversy between them in some sense, perhaps like a discharge of energy. At all events the abstract agreement, though unavoidable, is totally beyond comprehension, just as it is that two books can stand on exactly the same spot at the same moment, and helps us little in our present problem.

To the ultimates of these things, freedom and constancy, we cannot then look for a solution of the strife for when we look at them we merely find that there is no strife, they are not at strife but the strife between man and man continues.

Where then is situated this dilemma of man? If it is not in the ultimate truth then it must be in less than the ultimate truth, which condition is typified by ignorance. It is in association with ignorance then that this strife exists, perhaps even because of ignorance. To free him how shall we proceed? How else but by first seeing his errors, then by finding the truth and then by applying the truth to his errors? We will begin little, in detail, the better to grow up into generality and when we once have found something we think is true we shall expect to find it fit into a prepared place in existing things, and if it does not fit in this way we will not believe it to be true.

That I may not confuse myself unnecessarily with terms, I will take a familiar subject and proceed as follows: A man is constant to this thing. Since freedom depends upon knowledge, knowledge of truth, and since all "truth" we know is "natural law," [to] this natural law then we must look, we must investigate his condition as affected by natural law and if it, the law, bids him not be constant he cannot remain constant, but if law demand constancy he cannot exist except as constant. If he is to be free, then, law must command it and his freedom cannot be less than inevitable. But a law of such universal application as to general freedom must be general in its nature and the most general laws are the most abstract, so that here we expect to find that which will free men.

Now for a single case with common terms: A young man choosing his work. It is not conceived that any man would not know all the truth if he could and had the strength to bear it. But I cannot. Then where shall I proceed? Shall I do this or that? If I persist here I shall have no time to go there. Where then shall I go? For it is true that if I do not remain constant, if I do not go in one or another direction, I shall not go at all. Then I am not free but must blindly shut my eyes and yield to chance. "Agony, ignorance; nature the tyrant." No, let us look closer. There is still law; let us know and be free!

Surely if we do not remain constant we go nowhere, we are all false starts, we dissipate our energy, we have no economy. Economy! Economy then—is necessary. Economy is then not an end, not something to aim at so much as it is a law. And it is a general law, a very abstract one since applicable in so many diverse forms into which it enters as without a body of its own, thus being called abstract, so universally applicable. Perhaps this is the law we are looking for to free us.

Ah, but economy will not let me go where I want to—it will not let me go here—it is a tyrant! Then knowledge, a knowledge of this abstract thing has not conferred freedom but has merely bound us more and more. Our premise is likely false?

Let us trust this premise a little further however; let us seek freedom by gaining more knowledge—like a drunkard and his whiskey perhaps—let us go on; let us become more abstract. How does economy tyrannize? Why, the answer pants, I will be a sculptor, a poet, I will be an engineer, a lawyer, a ruler, but I cannot for I have not the capacity, says economy; that to do any I must do one only. Economy forbids, then it is a tyrant!

But if I do all am I really free? Is this freedom? Again I

ask wherein is this freedom I seek? We have conceived the essence of liberty to be to go forward under the truth we know, but the faster we go, the broader the truth, the freer we become. But if we do two things we have only half the time for each that we would have if we undertake only one, so that we go twice as slowly.

But if the truth in each of these things pursued is of a separate order, to neglect the one would be to invite ignorance, which is inconsistent with freedom. But if the truth in each be of the same nature and the same in fact, to do one of the two were greater freedom than to do the two, in which case economy were the greatest freedom and in no measure a tyrant. It seems that each pursuit is a language, it is as if we were to write a work in four different languages to desire to do all. The essence of the inspiration is the same, even the meter and form can be identical. These unifying abstract truths which underly all pursuits, then, were great things to find; we do not here seek them.

So then this economy, which limits to one thing, which is constancy, can imply freedom. Constancy is freedom! Here we have something very foolish or very fundamental and of utmost importance; for the division means, for instance, the beginning or end of monogamous marriage just as surely as that three and two make five.

Let us grant that it is true that freedom is constancy. How possibly can this be reasonable?

If the elemental truth is in all things, to [go] in five directions for one object is less quick and in a given time less true than to go in one direction—and truth, its knowledge, is necessary to freedom. Then constancy to one thing, leading us straightest by one path to truth is most freedom. If this be true it is well but it implies among other things that there is an equal abstract truth in all these various opportunities which I have called pursuits.

Then it is not to do this or that that is freedom for a man, but to do this thing to the greatest end, the nearer completeness, the farthest in one line. Thus in a piece of art or machinery, for a man to make one work embodying all his knowledge and power were better than a thousand pieces even a little less in knowledge and power than the one, but of course a thousand pieces of equally surpassing excellence were best of all.

If this be true, this likeness of freedom and constancy, we will expect, as we predicted we would, to find it familiarly applied in everyday intercourse. It must fit into its place or we will not believe it to be true.

In a man who is a painter, who by gross economy has been prevented from becoming a sculptor and poet as well, there is a tendency expressed in all the masters when their early and later works are compared to become more simple or as I believe more abstract, more general. That is he sees not trees and fence rails but horizontal and perpendicular lines, not an apple and a human face but crimson and a faint green shadow. But beyond that there are laws, even more abstract, that one rarely discovers, which may, in general, be classed as of that rhythm which bespeaks life. If what we have said is true, this artist's greatest laws are exactly those of the greatest sculptors and poets, and the painter is, in appreciation at least, a sculptor, a poet, so that Titian or Raphael, we would expect, could tell more of the truths of poetry than the most perfect rhymster and most intellectual in the handling of syllables: than a teacher of the whole art of poetics. For, this common truth, if we are correct, is not in the story, not in the colors, the marble or even in the ability to do; it is above, it is an abstraction. It is economy.

Thus we would expect to find in nature that the greatness of a man in one thing, should it be applied to other things, would also be great, and his weaknesses in the abstract are his weaknesses in the practical. Also that if he is limited in this art he is limited in that, so that his failure in collateral subjects would indicate the weak places which are bridged over in his principal art, so that Michael Angelo's sculpture may be robbed of its awe and seen more clearly by first reading his poetry and seeing his paintings. This all is of course based on abstract principle and not on expert adroitness.

By the abstract only, man is limited, and perfection tends to become more and more abstract. Facts and instances can be sought and explained, if possible, at will; nothing vouches for accuracy here.

So we come upon our generalities with which we have hoped to solve this controversy of freedom and constancy so wrecking to the lives of men. And we find that, granted a perfect abstract truth, no controversy exists. But until all be known it is both human and evident that the liberal of today will be the conservative of tomorrow. We are building; all is in degree; all is more or less conscious of the truth but until all knowledge be in our possession we must properly be divided into these sides. Also since the new may often be only a reversion and an error the liberal is rightly to be doubted and yet revered when honest, for the true liberal is the wiser man.

Yet, though in the dealings between man and man this can be true, the individual must live constant to one thing to be free, for paradoxical as it surely is, in this paradox lies his only liberty.

4. Love and Service

As far as any ultimate problem of the universe is concerned man on earth must forever be totally ignorant. For him all simply exists. He cannot know anything; he cannot even begin to know; he can merely appreciate; his sole possible activity can be but of two orders: to behold and to behold more. The why is unthinkable and action and will are merely corollaries of sight, not separate. Man is to thrill as the great horses of existence prance by him, he being one of them also, and to keep from being stepped on by knowing where the hoof will fall next. His only actions are to prance to cheer and to point, all of which are but one thing: praise.

When he does these things well, he prospers; when he does not do them well he is abolished in a flash or an eon, it is indifferent which, for both are equally sure. It is not what man will do except as he wills to see the inevitable in time to avoid calamity, will thus being merely an adjunct to sight, for laws are not merely puzzles but forces which mould and slay.

Thus to appreciate the law is well and man's proper part but the law's part is action, this is its object and the man who bears the broadest action of the law is most fit for its purposes, is most moulded to its inevitable way. Thus merely to live, to be affected now and here is the important thing and if it is well to live surely it is best to live fully, to enjoy to the full our life and to sorrow to the full over its loss. It is then to the warm sun we must go with eating and drinking and laughter after which if necessary to the very night with sorrow, between which comes wholesome sleep. Only that which is inevitable we have named "true," then fully, fully, not to excess which wastes and is not fully, but in an actual economy which wastes nothing.

But some will deny that it is our object merely to watch. Let me see. I am a watcher. Who do you esteem greater than I? A king? What has he? Lands. Good. What will he do with them? Eat them like a baby or roll in them like a horse? No, he will plant them with wheat and corn. But he cannot eat any more than he could before he planted, therefore these particular lands have not benefited him for he has more wheat than he wants already. What can he do but stand and watch others eat directly or indirectly by selling and buying. But this is a pleasure to him. Yes, but no greater than it is to me who stand by. But he has the pleasure of knowing that it is his property and his initiative that has performed the miracle. But it is the eating that I enjoy, to watch the eating directly or indirectly.

But the king is not embarrassed by circumstances, he can go about from place to place at will. For what purpose if not to see, to appreciate? For himself it is all less than nothing if he be too dull to appreciate or too sick to enjoy. The rest is futile.

Or else you may say: we live to work, to slave then. But it is certain that you do not live to slave to support children that they may work to support other children, that these may work and so forth indefinitely. This is no object; this is not your object but you live in the hope that you are slaving temporarily that you and others may not have to work so hard in the future, that you and they may have time to enjoy. This is your object and to enjoy is merely to look, to see, to appreciate through occupation or otherwise.

Or if you still think that life is something more than merely to look out at your eyes, as you may say, climb to the top of some mountain with a friend. You are arrived. What will you do or say? First, what is there to do? First to look and last merely to look. One is suddenly aroused from the ordinary diversions which surround him by the

isolation and simplicity of his position to find himself free
for a moment with beauty when with full force he sees the
end of all activity which has so suddenly culminated in this
moment. He finds no use for any formality he practices by
habit, all he knows how to do is mechanically rejected by
his mind until at last he is totally powerless in speech and
limb, his whole being given to sight, to appreciation. Then
comes a miracle, he has no satisfaction in his learned activi-
ties so at once he invents something new. He tries to sing,
he tries to dance, to speak praises in accordance with that
which he sees but, of course, fails. The point however is
that he tried to do a thing which had he been able he would
have done and that thing was to perform some act which
would symbolize the beauty he sees, reflect it and this is
expression, the outgrowth of sight, an act of appreciation,
praise. One wishes to be a poet, a painter, a something in-
stinctively known to be supreme, a something of which the
essence is sight in the broad sense, to include hearing, but
the reality he would express is silence. Our part is to watch
and to feel; we eat food merely for that.

It will be said now that this experience on the mountain
is perhaps truly exposed but that it is merely an incident in
life and not a consummation of its essential spirit; that this
experience is merely an eccentric moment and has no gen-
eral bearing on the object of activity in general. This is
totally wrong. The experience on the mountain typifies all
moments of intense feeling, of passion which we labor to
realize and which alone, as a promise, make labor endurable.
That is, these moments represent a summing up of the
effects of labor and so contain the efforts which precede
them which constitute routine life. In this way these mo-
ments have a most general bearing, in fact the most general
bearing as they hold in concentrated form the whole mean-
ing of the life which looks toward them and they are spent
as we have seen wholly in appreciation and praise.

Thus we live and eat merely to go about in the face of
wonder in the fullest glory of our senses only differing from

infants in a breadth of accomplishment and expression. We can do nothing but praise and what praise is there but fullest seeking after and enjoying?

This is praise. But still we must seek for forms by which to express, for we cannot, except in silence, praise direct, it must take a form and that form is beauty.

Oh, there will again be pageants, not empty shows but full of meaning, full of our spirit. There will be games praising by the perfection of our bodies. This is praise. And men shall come to the great altar of the Unknown with pomp and singing and processions and find there all the best, the truest, the most beautiful which shall be held up before them as a sign that man is seeing more and more.

That native was no fool who first praised the sun and the moon. We too shall have moon and sun feasts; we shall come to realize much that we now do not understand. Call this native an idolater, call him what you will. What is the moon to him? It is a light, a sign. He doesn't even know it is round. To him it is merely wonder, the unknown that is beautiful; to him it is an unconscious symbol which he used for praise. His, until perversion sets in through ignorance, is true expression, but you, you can see nothing but a dead sphere of clay which is not even true vision but half superstitious fancy, but the native sees beauty, wonder! You are the fool, not he. Or else what do you do that is better if you will not be called a fool? You have no beauty your own nor even a symbol of beauty except dead words, though there are many live ones, dead words which are symbols of symbols, twice removed from vitality—on a string like dried apples or Swedish bread. You are the idolaters, not the native. Oh you hypocrites, you shall yet kneel to the sun and moon and be cleaned.

We shall have the most beautiful before us; singing and architecture and painting and poetry, not as the dirty Cinderella of worship as it is now but as the thing itself. Man has always been unconsciously trying to associate these things with praise but there can be no association, for worship and beauty are an identity, thus so far we have failed. Go to Bach's Thomas Kirche in Leipzig if you will see this illustration in the life. First on Sunday there will come the hypocrites, tame of the tame through timidity ensuring the praise of virtue. You do not believe? Go on Saturday then, when the motets are being given free to all, when there is nothing but supremest music and there you will behold music. [Worship!] Can we not even see an indication of the identity of beauty such as music with praise by the intense heat awakened in the early fanatical puritans who opposed it, excluding this, and stained-glass windows with all other show from their churches? What else but some such great reality could awake such supreme and vigorous opposition even to the point of martyrdom against it? This is a sure sign of its vitality and truth.

But two things we must avoid. We must not forget that we praise the unknown, the mystery about which nothing can be said; and second, that we praise in silence, the rest being but perishable signs. Then lest we mistake our signs for the reality let them be ever new, forever new for only by forever changing the sign can we learn to separate from it its meaning, the expression from the term, and so cease to be idolaters.

For I could live forever in a hut in a valley and if I were born there I would mistake the valley for peace, the hut for comfort, my dog for love, one flower for beauty and myself for king of creation just as has been done many times in the past. Therefore I travel. Manners that differ, customs, worships that differ show that no language, no custom, no worship is the truth but the truth is a formless thing which lies in them as within a suit of clothes, in part. Then I see that I must be forever new lest I become an idolater in my valley, but I would be the biggest fool imaginable if I took my valley to express nothing. Then comes death to relieve me, it is imaginable, of the greatest hypocrisy of all, as any hero will tell, that this world is life for, living, as with truth, is also a thing without body and expressed here merely.

We have so far conspicuously neglected one thing, love. As this is part of life and since we find life to be merely to see and to express, then love must be definable in terms of sight and expression. It is merely this: alone I enjoy, with another I enjoy, that is, praise (in essence) twofold. But to be one with all creatures is to enjoy perhaps beyond the limits of thought. There is then no more nor no less in love than this: To watch together, to sing together. It is still the same: to walk about, but not alone.

But why the peculiar love of man and woman?

That which is still strong needs no protection, but that which is weak needs protection, but that which is weakest needs most protection. The inevitable, such as death, needs no urging, but the special purpose, such as life, must be protected. So it is easy for man to die but for the inscrutable reason he is to live, therefore he is protected by his strongest instincts of passion. These are merely devices to prolong life therefore to prolong sight and praise to which they are secondary as a part. And though love enters in with them in some cases love has no part with passion but as passion is less and less useful, love shines more and more out, if it be there at all. In fact the purest love is between men and men and women and women: between old and young and in fact under all such conditions of love by which passion is excluded.

The illustration of all this is before us each day.

Look at lovers if you have never been one. It is a mere repetition of the experience on the mountain for this simple reason, that this is one of the intense, consummate moments which contain more heat than others. They remain silent together for hours. Two brothers, I mean, or sweetheart and man if you choose. Let them rarely try to talk or when they do solely impassionately with the beauty of conviction, for though this be wonderful praise their treasure is silence, let them merely look, for this is their treasure.

Now, however passion has subsided or been glutted and the lie that it has acted, that it is love, bursts the two apart or else horrible decay sets in. However, in another case, love indeed has existed. Watch these two through the first ecstatic years. They go still side by side, peculiarly contented. It is love itself they now find that is lovely. Each becomes an unconscious symbol in the other's eyes, a symbol of love which is beautiful, but mistaking the symbol for the reality they overlook deformity and misery or else at last through ignorance become cynics. This is the very commonest phenomenon of all. From the beginning of time, or of history at least, one has seen love, but trying to describe it, describes the symbol and in that love is so much greater than its terms finds it impossible not to magnify, impossible not to think that here, in the symbol, is the greatest beauty of all. But often this symbol is suddenly destroyed when we see at last that love is not anything mortal, that it flows over the forms of the world like water that comes and withdraws. Yet as the objects of life are all we can know love by, this coming and going discloses us to be involved in a destiny more than we can imagine, which must be very marvelous.

Thus sight in its intensity has given us a joy, now it gives us a sorrow which is pity for if I see far and feel deeply how can I fail to see the misery of men? But how unnecessary it is, for if I saw that it was necessary I would not pity but I would go my own way. But because these people can be well I pity them and do not pity a stone. Now comes service.

But how shall I serve? I cannot love these people as they are for I cannot love dirt and laziness and ignorance—merely by loving life which is what they might be. For after I have rid myself of the encumbrances which hold me from going about freely and which the hungry are eager for, that is, money, etc., what is there left for me to do? Is my service at end? And when, since it is unnecessary, therefore doomed to extinction by simple economy, there is no more an object for pity, am I reduced to an absolute inability to serve? All this shows that service in the common sense is no service at all but a device which would, if there were perception present at the same time, prepare a man for service. "For life is to walk about, to see, which is to feel, to express," as we have said, or in sum, to give praise, to put into form what we see which is our only service.

Service is not to humbly put the head under the knife for any first indiscriminate prisoner but to believe proudly in love as a law and to stand for this clear intellectual belief permanently, so that a form be given to the reality in your own person, than which there is no greater praise, which it solely is. And when the form is destroyed the permanent shines out for the first time clearly. Personally what is it to me if I see the end of life and keep from speaking of it. Or if when I am told to cease, I cease? What is it to know this thing in my heart merely? For if the mere knowledge were all to me, might I not cease to speak or speak of other things? But the knowledge I have is in itself nothing; I must give it, I must love. I will, in fact, tell it against my very life itself, by which I make love greater than life, greater than knowledge. For it goes beyond life, where no knowledge goes and is the most daring of all the mysteries and the most wonderful, which is a sufficient pretext for the presence here of man.

5. Waste and Use

NATURE'S final command is: "Do not waste." Insofar as life is to do, it is: "Do not waste time." Insofar as life is to see, it is: "Do not waste space." Thus we see that life is to confine our energy and for us to expand our view. Which, again, shows that a perfection is the object of our activity, any perfection which alone at once contains a universal expansion concentrated into a minimum of elements constituting it for in a perfection is no waste. This principle also shows that to reach this perfection we must be at it continually, thus not wasting time but looking about completes our endeavor by showing that the thing we perfect is not the perfection but perishable and the more we look the more we become convinced of this, thus fulfilling both commands in our effort.

This "command of nature"; this universal abstract principle we name economy. Sparing may not be economy but fullest effort always is. Economy is simply using to the full; it is simply using anything to the most complete advantage.

This desired object of economy has been obtained by system, but all systems are only partial unless they include all nature, but nature itself is above all, systematic, so that this must be our final economy: to know all the laws and to use them. That is, we must not make a system, but we must discover the system. Yet temporarily we must use the incomplete system we know, correcting and amplifying continually.

Thus we can say that ignorance, since it ignores laws it cannot know, is always poor economy and since dirt seems dependent upon ignorance, personal filthiness I mean, why then dirt must be poor economy. Then it is economy to be clean and if it is economy it is law and inevitable if we will survive. This is a mere example.

And so all excess is plainly poor economy.

Thus all our life is, materially as we alone know it, compelled toward a more and more perfect use, a perfect economy, but as with all laws in their perfection the perfect economy is expressed only in beauty. And it is certain that purity which we require in woman is nothing more nor less either than the beautiful flower of the common plant, economy. And all that is manly—all doing, perseverence, daring, courage, all are nothing else than economy in their reduction, however we glamour them about. It is all: the set value, the single path, concentration of energy, each is economy of purpose which alone makes action beautiful.

Waste is the only real danger, just as there is no real difference between monogamy and polygamy, aside from ignorant, uneconomical, prejudice, except that the passion has been forced into a saving habit. One alternative is good and the other poor economy. And yet this law which alone can determine the orbit of stars is seen as a small thing and merely applied to managing houses and countries, it is unromantic.

Thus among several reasons given by a man for my choosing to live alone with this woman, these reasons being intended to be very ironical, is that I am too lazy to go about for others. This is the sole reason.

Were I as big as a river there would be no argument if one asked me to be contained in a cup, but being about cup large I can fill only one cup, of more or less adaptable dimensions. I do not conceive myself as being copious enough to give myself fully to more than one and finding it necessary to give or take, if you will, once fully rather than twice partially I am by necessity too lazy to be divided by overmultiplication.

Perhaps as I progress in capacity, as woman will also, I mean in the year 1,011,000 A.D. we will be river large. But if such a gap as that between the present woman and the then man could exist, even for a generation, and I were that man, I think in that case I could be content with a thousand women of proper assortment.

To do, then, to the full. Man is limited in power and is subject to fatigue. It is a mathematical certainty that he can only do a given amount of work of a set quality in a certain time. If he does more in amount it is of smaller worth and evens up in this way on the quantity. Therefore rest, which may take the form of play, is economy and with more rest we would, in the overworked, expect better quality of thought.

Man can only work with his body, including the brain. To use this and perfect it is essential and he that neglects it must be of less value than another who does not and therefore must perish, for it will be believed that only out of a perfect body can come complete use.

The best is the fullest we can do but this best we are forced to do, we must do it. To attack one thing with fullest energy but with clear eyes is all one man can do. This then is best for him, and fullest energy means concentration. But what shall he attack? Here is the solution of the problem of education. If he show a tendency, recognize it first then make this a unifying motive and cluster information as far-reaching as possible around it, putting forward strongly its antitheses also. Build strongly on the natural structure as on a solid foundation.

But if he have no special aptitude or inclination, what shall he attack? What shall I attack? That which presents itself or anything. The thing next your hand. If he does not know where to divide between two things, attack either. One will be truth the other lie or else indifferent. With concentration, energy, with periods of rest, go to the end with either. The laws are solid. What is the result? If he has struck the lie with open eyes he is by the very energy of his attack flung back from it into the true, merely mechanically and just so hard as he has attacked so much the more clearly will his doubt be ended. But if he have no eyes he may acquire them or else let him go on, if he is not a coward, that is a poor economist, keep on hard and by his very energy he will be the quicker destroyed and the lie correct itself. Yet if he be in the trail of truth the more his energy, the more his advance. And fullest energy cannot be anything but fullest economy; neither under nor over use.

Thus in the pursuit of law, coarse or fine, truth or beauty, material or immaterial, the deed is the turning point, the nucleus of conflict, and its value is in assertion, praise, no matter what its aim happens to be. The deed is a fixed base on which sight may stand for the next step, the next leap in either or any direction. Yet it is also certain that the mere deed, regardless of its quality, is not the completeness of action merely by its intensity, but the deed, even to its creator is in itself entirely worthless except as a crude model of that shape which he wills shall later contain the truth of beauty. This essence, if it come to dwell in his deed, is its lasting value.

Thus we have said that the deed is in itself not of worth by its intensity, its economy, but by its content of beauty-truth, and this seems reasonable. But now we will say, and mark it, that knowledge has no absolute value and all the value it has exists in the deed. This is not a paradox. Look and see why, but first I must test the second statement above.

Knowledge we say is in itself purely without worth for if it were a value intrinsically, the more of it gained, by mathematical progression, would increase the total worth of the thing containing it. In this case a school boy today is immeasurably a more valuable thing than Pythagoras ever was because he knows of laws and has them at his finger tips, which Pythagoras could never possess. In this way the best of our best men now alive is of less value than the worst of the worst man in some future age when knowledge is so advanced that the worst has a greater quantity of knowledge than our present best. We are then totally tyrannized over by the accident of our time and are totally unable to free ourselves, for we can never overcome our disadvantages, our best is absolutely insignificant in the face of infinity and once we are overcome by the succeeding generations our personal, intrinsic value is nil. We have transferred our knowledge, but by so doing have become useless and void forever or until some cataclysm abolishes all knowledge above us and we again contain more knowledge than the beasts.

Granting, then, that knowledge has no absolute worth, let us search out its relative one since it surely has some value.

We at once see that the gaining of knowledge has typified the prominent men of all ages, supreme among whom are such singers as Homer. Then if knowledge has no real worth what remains but the effort to gain it? If in the effort and the accomplishment the worth is contained, then one age is as free as another and the man who creates his object with this completeness is equal to the man who wins his knowledge with an equal perfection ten thousand years later or earlier, and knowledge only, merely points us to the pain and plaster. We thus have a very valuable point for criticism of our time, for though men now live to progress they should reverse the order of their object and progress merely to live.

But knowledge is thought to be infinite so that forever we may have and have always been able to have intrinsic greatness. Thus we find in the deed a worth that stretches into all ages and is personal, vigorous, constructive, but that the fruit is as with all other fruit merely the seed of its own kind, it is merely sight and freedom for further effort and nothing more. For work does not lead to peace but to more work and therein lies the prize.

Thus we have knowledge become money by which we purchase deeds and in the deed, if we are correct, lies the value, though the deed itself is worthless. Thus we see that knowledge and the thing known are entirely separate.

Now let the difference be settled if possible. If worth be the same in deeds in all ages and it rest on the content of beauty-truth in a deed, the conclusion is inevitable that there is more or less beauty in this complete simple and complete complex object, and an equal worth must exist in the perfect simple as in the perfect complex, and as little worth in the imperfect simple as in the imperfect complex. But when man begins to be an idolater before the simple, knowledge rescues him by presenting the complicated, for the disillusion which he must continually have, but the value is the indestructible and unchanged, the perfection.

So life, then, is to do where I am, to the fullest of my power, with clear eyes which tell me plainly that it is neither possible nor desirable to do all but that my best is all that I can do. It seems that I must search in one line for laws and all the while live conscious in the face of mystery but glad in the fullest power of the sense. Glad to live also.

I must be ready to go anywhere at any time, faithfully, at the command of the true, but when I am bidden there will be little doubt as to direction, the call is as distinct as birth.

Notes

p. 9 (last two paras.): In the original typescript this passage reads as follows:

This seems to be the characteristic American *position* of the intelligence—the pioneer turn of mind—the individual superior to authority. No external it connotated by our history, temperament—the one profitably to be observed. (referring to the chapters to follow) No attempt is made to correlate them except in so far as to relate them back the original indirect *position,* outside of "learning." The European mediaval aspiration toward a peak, aristocratic striving: the American toward a useful body of knowledge made to serve the individual who is *primary.*

p. 12 (par. 2): "Scholards" may be a slip of Williams's pen, or an error by his typist, but the resulting portmanteau word (scholardullard) is too good to edit out.

p. 13 (par. 5): "Thought is not writing, to write betrays both writing and itself." *Sic.* The infinitive "to write" lacks an object. "Thought" seems the most likely possibility, *i.e.,* ". . . to write [thought] betrays both writing and itself."

p. 14 (par. 5): "He stands outside the thought which encloses his work not in 'thoughts' their trouble." *Sic.* It's impossible to tell what Williams intended here.

p. 19: ". . . thus reasserting their own powerful   and by blasting away . . ." *Sic.* The blank space appears in the typescript.

p. 24: Williams's discussion of Cézanne and of the artist's perception in general can be usefully compared with Rollo May's in *Love and Will:*

The new world which Cézanne reveals is characterized by a transcendence of cause and effect . . . all aspects of the forms are born in on our vision simultaneously—or not at all. . . . The painting is mythic, not literalistic or realistic. . . . And most important of all, I cannot even *see* the painting if I stand totally outside it; it communicates only if I *participate* in it. I cannot see Cézanne by observing his rocks as an accurate rendering of rocks,

193

but only . . . as patterns of forms which speak to me through my own body and my feelings and perceptions of my world.

Merleau-Ponty, in his essay, "Cézanne's Doubt," also calls attention to this bodily quality of the artist's vision.

p. 25: "If he can record that with (and it is always a problem of) mastery and material. . . ." In the typescript Williams closes the parenthesis after "material."

p. 26 (par. 3): "Its" in the first sentence should be corrected to "their." I've let it stand because Williams obviously thinks of "science-and-philosophy" as a unit taking a singular possessive.

p. 33: The numbering here follows the typescript. I don't know whether the missing passages were lost or deleted. The notation after "4" "(insert Dot bit)," addressed either to himself or to his typist, suggests that the missing passages were lost. The "Dot bit" has not been located.

p. 35 (par. 1): "Reflect" should be corrected to "reflection," but it's also possible that Williams intended the word to have the force of a verb.

p. 36 (par. 1): In the typescript Williams closes the parenthesis after "entities."

p. 37 (last par.): ". . . the direct object of scholarship that is the but, but clarity . . ." *Sic.* The four words immediately following "scholarship" might be deleted without doing violence to the sentence. However, Williams seems to be using the first "but" in the sense of "goal" or "objective," as the French announce a goal in soccer: "*But!*" In one of his earliest poems, "To My Better Self" (*Poems,* 1909), he uses the word this way. "Sure your purposed but should be to live in our commend."
"I use the [quotation marks] . . ." The typescript reads: "I use the parenthesis . . ."

p. 43: In the typescript this page is preceded by a page containing only the following title and notations: "The New in Art and its Significance. 10 Chapters—the Chapters beginning Every 5 pages—Bits of conversation copied in." I've omitted the page entirely, to avoid giving the false impression that it is the title page of a separate section of the whole text.

p. 46: In his *Autobiography* (pp. 20–21) Williams tells in detail the story of trampling the farmer's grain, being caught and beaten.

p. 49: "And thus before the mind goes always—and by necessity—the imagination." *Cf. Kora in Hell,* XVIII, 1:

The act is disclosed by the imagination of it. But of first importance is it to realize that the imagination leads and the deed comes behind. First Don Quixote then Sancho Panza.

p. 53 (par. 2): "Man must give himself without complete knowledge in the world. . ." *Cf.* Keats's letter on "Negative Capability."

p. 59: The last sentence in the second paragraph might be emended to read: "So, far more logically, I assume the man as fixed [whom] knowledge must approach by proofs of his terms or be rejected as wholly illogical and beside the point."

pp. 62–63: Throughout this section Williams is alluding directly and indirectly to *The Education of Henry Adams.* See especially the chapter "The Dynamo and the Virgin" in Adams's *Education.*

p. 64: The two numbered sentences are either paraphrased or misquoted from *The Education of Henry Adams.* Williams often seems to quote from memory, without double-checking the accuracy of his citation.

p. 66: "Music" is the subject of the last copula in the final sentence of paragraph 1, which might be emended to read: "It [*i.e.,* poetry] caps music which fails where it seems just at the point of success, and most expressive, by its inarticulateness, requiring the words of songs; as the poetry gains just that expressiveness which music serves at the same time, but [music, as it serves the poetry,] is never heightened [to be] more articulate."

pp. 68–69: Throughout this section Williams seems to be "thinking out loud" on paper, making some false starts, then backing up to begin again. I've left the text as it stands, to give the flavor of his notes.

p. 72 (par. 3): The "series" mentioned here may be the same as that sketched briefly above (p. 66).

p. 73 (par. 2): "Unity" and "multiformity" are further allusions to *The Education of Henry Adams.*

p. 74 (par. 4): For "define" in the opening sentence read "distinguish."

p. 78 (par. 3): See above (p. 46 and note) on getting caught in a wheatfield.

p. 80 (par. 5): The "saying of Juan Gris" is quoted above (p. 52).

p. 80 (par. 7): The metaphor of a "universal (donator)" may be taken from Williams's medical practice. People with Type O blood are called "universal donors" because their blood can be safely transfused into patients with any blood type.

p. 81 (par. 1): The verb "are" following the parenthesis in the final sentence of this paragraph should be corrected to "is," predicate of the singular subject "all that halts us." But clearly Williams intends a compound subject—"all that halts us," "accumulations" and "books."

p. 84 (last par.): It's difficult to tell whether Williams intended to write ". . . what he says is scientific and scientifically true," or, omitting the repetition entirely, ". . . what he says is scientifically true." I've allowed the text to stand as it is.

p. 85 (par. 3): "(L)" might stand for Wyndham Lewis, of whom Williams speaks in the preceding paragraph.

p. 98 (par. 3): The notation "(from R)" *might* indicate "from Rx pads." Williams often wrote notes and even whole poems on his prescription blanks.

p. 100 (par. 4): The last sentence *might* be emended to read: "He was a homeless, sexless, origin-less mind that, being almost without education of any kind, but of large size and heady flow, took on, in a mould that solely suited it and came ready, the only thing it could, the actual shape of lives."

p. 102 (par. 1): The last sentence might be emended to read: "I doubt very much if arguing from the work the condition (which is a living state of the imagination, superior to any of the parts of high scholarship) could be arrived at."

p. 106 (par. 3): "It is—in that it is wholly for himself, to himself— impersonal the only impersonal." *Sic.* It's hard to tell what Williams intended here, but the sentence might be emended to read: ". . . wholly for himself, to himself—impersonal, the only impersonal."

p. 112 (lines 4–5): The two quoted lines are from *Cymbeline.*

p. 112 (last par.): "Thomasian" *Sic.* Read "Thomistic."

p. 117 (par. 4): "the Shaw's, the Welles's." The typescript reads: "the Shows, the Wells."

p. 120 (par. 8): The demonstratives ("these," "this") are confusing, but the sense is not inaccessible. Creative minds and "Morgan's" (*i.e.,* the wealthy) are jealous of each other and these jealousies (on both sides) defeat support. The jealousies "prevent endowment." The antecedent of the pronoun "it" in the final sentence is not all clear—the creative mind? or the moment?

p. 122 (title): Cf. above (p. 116), where Williams uses this phrase in connection with Gertrude Stein.

p. 123 (par. 4): In the typescript the last two sentences read: "Today it is the end of science. Whose unrelated conclusions are falsely applied to every situation in life to which they are whether they are alien or otherwise."

p. 125 (par. 1): "The skeleton" may be a further allusion to his earlier use of this phrase in connection with Gertrude Stein (pp. 116 and 122).

p. 129 (par. 8): "From prestige, as its lack poetry is surely now lower than ever." *Sic.* The sentence might be emended to read: "From prestige, as lacking it, poetry is surely now lower than ever."

p. 130 (par. 4): ". . . from place, a place, begins everything—is in fact a place. Synchronously occupied by everything and at the same time space itself—nothing but." *Cf.* Alfred North Whitehead, *Science and the Modern World:*

> The unity of the perceptual field therefore must be a unity of bodily experience . . . my theory involves the entire abandonment of the notion that simple location is the primary way in which things are involved in space-time. In a certain sense, everything is everywhere at all times. For every location involves an aspect of itself in every other location. Thus every spatio-temporal standpoint mirrors the world. [Free Press paperback edition, p. 91]

In *A Novelette* (written in 1929 and published in 1932) Williams makes a similar statement: "So all things enter into the singleness of the moment and the moment partakes of the diversity of all things." (*Imaginations*, p. 282) Williams had read Whitehead's book in 1927. (See *Selected Letters*, pp. 79, 85.)

p. 131 (par. 1): The possessive pronoun "his" in the first sentence refers to the "man" implicit in the phrase "human history" earlier in the same sentence. It is perhaps revealing that Williams doesn't say "our" rather than "his."

p. 133 (par. 7): "That is the basis—not order is some charm in itself." *Sic.* I can think of three possible emendations: (1) "That [*i.e.,* place] is the basis—not [that] order is some charm in itself." (2) "That is the basis—not order [in] some charm in itself." (3) ". . . not order [as] some charm in itself."
  On the preceding pages Williams writes "conscience" when he obviously intends "conscious" or "consciousness," and I've silently emended the text in those two instances. Here his intention is less clear and I've allowed the text to stand as it is in the typescript.

p. 134 (par. 1): ". . . the [initiation] into whatever system. . ." The typescript reads: ". . . the inition into whatever system. . ."

p. 135 (last par.): "Anomatic" *Sic.* It may be that Williams is deriving this adjective from the French *anomie,* "without name" or "without measure."

"Appraised" *Sic.* Williams might have intended "praised."

p. 136 (par. 3): "Congregate" *Sic.* Williams might have intended "congruous" or "congregated."

p. 137 (par. 2): Cf. the chapter "Père Sebastian Rasles" in Williams's *In the American Grain,* in which Williams himself is pictured as the "unscholarly gist" which the French scholar Valéry Larbaud studies in order to understand America.

p. 146 (bottom): A word has obviously been omitted between "great" and "lies." The most likely emendation seems to be: ". . . a great [opportunity] lies for correcting. . ."

p. 148: In the typescript these quotes and the dedication appear at the top of the page on which the next chapter, ["The Pluralism of Experience"], begins. I've placed them on a page of their own here, to separate them from any individual essay, and I've also reproduced them in the front matter, where it seems to me obvious Williams intended them to appear.

p. 164 (par. 2): "All nature now becomes a symbol for me to use." Cf. Emerson's essay, "Nature" (1836).

p. 166 (par. 3): A word has obviously been omitted between "extremely" and "one."

p. 168 (par. 2): "And if all truth contains everything, why, is not this world a part of the whole truth. . ." Cf. Wallace Stevens's poem, "Landscape with Boat."

p. 172 (par. 3): The typescript reads: "My ignorance, not law, is the tyrant for now that I know how to fly there is no law to prevent me from doing so. ('—for doing. This 'doing' is good.)"

p. 175 (par. 5): ". . . and truth, it's knowledge, is necessary to freedom." *Sic.* It's difficult to tell whether Williams intended to write "and truth, its knowledge. . . ." or whether he intended the "it's" as a contraction, so that the sentence migh be emended to read: ". . . and truth, [it is] knowledge, is necessary. . ."

p. 182 (par. 1): ". . . and there you will behold music. [Worship!]" In the typescript "Worship!" is written in longhand above the line.

p. 183 (par. 1): ". . . with another I enjoy, that is, praise (in essence) twofold." In the typescript the sentence reads: ". . . with another I enjoy twofold." Written in longhand, above the line, Williams has inserted: "that is praise (in essence)."